DISCIPLINE WITH PURPOSE

Nurturing a Child's Self-Discipline

A Program for Adults Working with Children Pre-K through Ninth Grade

Barbara C. Vasiloff, M.A.

Discipline with Purpose: Nurturing a Child's Self-Discipline

ISBN: 978-1-7345028-0-0

Front Cover Image: 123rf.com/rawpixel
Back Cover Images: 123rf.com/bowie15

Kara Scrivener, Editor

www.emergingink.com

Notice: The information in this book is true and complete to the best of our knowledge. It is offered without guarantee on the part of the author, the editor/formatter, or the book's press. The author disclaims all liability in connection with the use of this book.

Dedication

This book is dedicated to the late Dr. Laurel N. Tanner whose educational theories and research were used to develop the self-discipline skills framework used in the *Discipline with Purpose* program, and the late P.M. Forni, co-founder of the John Hopkins Civility Project who identified the daily actions deemed necessary to form a civil society.

Table of Contents

Acknowledgements

Many people were instrumental in developing the concept of self-discipline outlined in this book. They never wavered in their dedication to the belief that all children have the capacity to pursue their dreams when they are self-disciplined.

In the early years of development, Monsignor John A. Flynn, former Director of Education for the Omaha Catholic Archdiocese, encouraged us to devote time and energy to research best practices in education and share our work through national speaking engagements.

Educators, Diane Flynn, M.A. in guidance and counseling; Dr. Elizabeth Kearney Gross, PhD in education; Judy Kulp, elementary school administrator; Jan Quint, masters in behavioral studies; and parent Lynn Murtagh conducted training sessions and spoke with authenticity about their experiences with the *DWP* process. They were able to share first-hand stories illustrating successful results.

I owe thanks to my niece Christine Ryktarsyk who allowed us to use her delightful poems and to Jo Mersnick, who created the lyrics to the skill songs. Hundreds of teachers field-tested lesson plans and created assessments, songs, posters, skill illustrations, and activities for physical education, art, and computer classes. They identified children's literature that focused on self-discipline.

The first administrator to adopt the 15 skills identified in *Discipline with Purpose* as a way of life for members of the school community was Sr. Jean Perry, C.S.A. former principal of Precious Blood Elementary School in Fort Wayne, Indiana. Precious Blood has been a *DWP* school since 1984.

Friends and family members helped to prepare this manuscript. My brother-in-law John Przybocki and long-time friend Ruth Tempelmann edited the first draft. Readers who offered suggestions and made the second and third drafts possible include Joan Riggert, Michael Reitz, Jan Zigler, Suzanne Hartman, and editor Kimberly Crum.

Immeasurable gratitude goes to Paula Lenz, MS in Education and Technology, teaching partner, and co-founder of *Discipline with Purpose* and to her husband Vince who first shared with us Tanner's book

Classroom Discipline and encouraged us along the way. Paula's insights, expertise, and realistic view of teaching offset my idealism and allowed us to develop a well-balanced program.

Preface

When I was young, most days ended with our parents asking us to share the best and the worst of the days' happenings. My brother, two sisters, and I spoke about new friends, mean kids, teachers we loved, and those we tolerated. Some days we admitted our poor choices. We made our confessions and vowed not to repeat those actions. Of course, we didn't always remember to keep those promises. What we did remember was that someone cared about our day, guided our choices, and helped us be responsible for our decisions.

Thinking about our behavior was an integral part of life. My parents used common phrases to discipline us: "Go to your room and think about what you did. I'll be in shortly to find out how you plan to fix it. If you are not feeling guilty about what you did, you should be. Guilt means you understand that you have hurt someone. I understand that you are sorry, but what will you do to show that sorrow?" Our parents praised us when we acted responsibly. The best moments came when they pointed out positive actions. They told us they were proud when we used our social skills to help a neighbor. They complimented us on our ability to converse with adults who joined us for dinner. We did not realize our parents were training us to be self-disciplined.

In 1978, after serving as a visiting professor at Benedictine College in Atchison, Kansas, I took a job teaching at the high school level at Father Flanagan's Boys Town in Omaha, NE. Father Edward J. Flanagan established Boys Town in 1917 as a safe haven for boys who needed care. He believed "true, lasting learning was best accomplished through kindness, care, and concern and not through fear of pain and punishment" (Boys Town: Saving Children, Healing Families, n.d.).

My co-teacher at the time was Paula Lenz. Before coming to Boys Town, Paula worked in inner city schools. She dealt with students who struggled to get to school on time, believed they didn't need to be in school, and frequently challenged authority. In her teaching, following school rules and discipline took center stage.

I knew private schools from the inside, having taught both elementary and secondary students for over 15 years. At that time, the majority of my students were from homes where respect for authority was taught. Disciplinary issues were less dramatic and included nominal infractions such as being out of uniform, late to class, and not finishing work. Yet, children who were receptive to schooling could sit in classrooms for eight months without being challenged to develop discipline skills beyond rule keeping.

Paula and I loved the Boys Town environment – the students, faculty, and the family-teachers who lived with the boys and then the girls when they began attending the school in 1979. However, we struggled with the behavior modification system that the home used to discipline students. We rejected using a memorized script, as the program dictated, to help older students manage their behaviors. Students often mocked the script and showed they knew how to 'play the game.' We thought the script developmentally inappropriate.

Our weekly department meetings often led to the topic of discipline. We combed the current literature, reading the works of Robert and Isabel Hawley, Dr. James Dobson, Rudolf Dreikurs and Pearl Cassel, Kevin Swick, Eugene Howard, Charles Wolfgang and Carl Glickman, Richard Curwin and Allen Mendler, Thomas Good, Thomas Biddle, and Jere Brophy.

One day, Paula's husband, a guidance counselor, gave us the book *Classroom Discipline* (1978) by Dr. Laurel Tanner, Professor at Temple University in Philadelphia. Dr. Tanner had developed 12 principles of classroom discipline. Five of these principles seemed most relevant:

1. The aims of education and classroom discipline are the same: to help children and youth become self-directed persons.
2. Discipline is inseparable from teaching.
3. Discipline should change with the child's stage of development and help him/her move to the next step.
4. Socialization requires the redirection of destructive behavior into socially useful behavior.
5. Ways of dealing with misbehavior should be consonant with developmental goals.

Tanner observed that educators often taught compliance, but few taught self-discipline. This resonated with us. Our college coursework had included classroom management and methods for dealing with out-of-bounds behaviors, but neither of us had received training that dealt directly with self-discipline. We learned from Dr. Tanner that there was no developed curriculum for teaching self-discipline. In the *Phi Delta Kappan* magazine, Tanner wrote:

> For university professors, those who study and write about problems of education, discipline is not a problem of great importance. If it were, the professional literature would reflect that concern. Substantial scientific research on classroom discipline is rare... The proper education of teachers must include a developmental approach to discipline in which discipline is linked to the purposes of education (1981, p. 494-497).

We wondered if there was a way to teach self-discipline that could begin as soon as children entered kindergarten.

When we created the *Discipline with Purpose* program, there was no established norm for defining self-discipline; nor was there a way to measure student growth in self-discipline. Students embodied a wide variety of value systems. Faculty members in our individual schools had their own value systems. We wondered what would happen if parents and educators agreed to adopt a similar framework for teaching self-discipline and maintain that framework through a child's first nine years of schooling. What would happen if we taught self-discipline developmentally as one might teach other subjects? What would happen if we challenged students to self-evaluate their progress in developing self-discipline skills? What would happen if parents and educators used a shared vocabulary when discussing appropriate and inappropriate behaviors? These were the questions our program sought to answer.

In the past 35 years, Paula and I have had the privilege of meeting with thousands of public and private school educators and parents in 36 states across the U.S. We designed our seminars to not only discuss self-discipline techniques that could be taught to children from kindergarten through ninth grade, but to encourage teachers and parents alike to become aware of the value of such skills. In 1984, we founded *Discipline with Purpose: A Developmental Approach to Teaching Self-Discipline.*

Attendees at our training workshops often asked for a reference book containing the ideas presented. Until now, our answer was, "It's in the works." Finally, the history, assumptions, development, goals, strategies, and some activities used in the *Discipline with Purpose* program are being recorded. The audience for this book includes administrators, classroom educators, youth leaders, future educators, and parents home-schooling their children.

Paula and I are more convinced today than we were 35 years ago that teaching learners how to become self-disciplined is essential. The 15-skills framework identified in *Discipline with Purpose* has endured the test of time. All or part of the 15 skills have been incorporated in contemporary educational programs. Such programs as Positive Behavior Interventions and Supports, Social Emotional Learning, Responsive Classrooms, and Restorative Justice recognize the importance of teaching social emotional skills. In the past 15 years, scientific research has validated children's need to learn these skills. Duckworth and Seligman have confirmed that self-discipline, unlike IQ, correlates more strongly to academic success in a variety of areas and is a better predictor of achievement over the school year (2005).

Decades have passed since our program began. Children still need guidance to learn the skills that will make them successful adults. Adults still need to know successful ways to nurture a child's self-discipline.

"Children cannot become self-disciplined unless they are taught. They cannot be taught unless adults are knowledgeable and intentionally teach the skills. Adults can convey to children that they too are learning how to become better at practicing self-discipline. When self-discipline skills are taught, children can learn to be civil and the skills can build an intrinsic incentive in children to help them fulfill their goals and dreams."

Barbara Vasiloff, M.A., President and Co-founder of *Discipline with Purpose*

Introduction

How *Discipline with Purpose* Began

When I began teaching, I knew I would need to discipline. Yet, I was uncomfortable confronting misbehavior and unsure of how to make every punishment fit the crime, as conventional wisdom taught. I hoped my classroom would fill with students who had already mastered self-control. While I maintained an orderly classroom and structured class time to discourage misbehavior, I continued to search for information that would teach me the art and the science of discipline. For this reason, the book *Classroom Discipline* by Tanner made an impact. Her challenge to teachers was to do more than discipline children – teach them self-discipline. Intrigued with this concept, my co-teacher Paula Lenz and I phoned Dr. Tanner to inquire how self-discipline could be taught. Dr. Tanner advised, "You know, I sit here in my ivory tower and write about theories. You are the practitioners and need to find the answer." She invited us to use her research.

Dr. Tanner studied the skills students need to function well in a classroom. She noted approximate ages when children can perform tasks without prompts or cues from an adult. She reported that, not until the end of the second grade, are most students able to follow more than three verbal instructions.

By fourth grade, children can distinguish between situations in which they must raise hands to speak and situations in which they can offer ideas in a free-flowing discussion. She cautioned, when children are not taught how to follow instructions or how to discern appropriate behavior based on the situation, their actions can be perceived as a discipline problem rather than a lack of skill due to their developmental phase.

Dr. Tanner suggested that we consider the following points as we explored a way to teach self-discipline:

- Clearly and simply distinguish between discipline, punishment, and self-discipline.

- Describe/define self-discipline so that even a five-year-old could understand the concept.
- Identify specific skills that a self-disciplined person can exhibit.
- Create a developmentally appropriate, experiential curriculum.
- Consider teaching self-discipline just like you might teach other subjects.
- Discover unique ways to motivate children to practice self-discipline.
- Require students to self-assess their progress in becoming self-disciplined.

Armed with these guidelines, our 30 years of combined teaching experience, and a strong desire to succeed, Paula and I began developing the *Discipline with Purpose* program.

I am forever grateful to Dr. Tanner and her work. As we developed *DWP*, Paula and I continued to correspond with her through letters and phone conversations. As the years passed, we lost touch. I never had the privilege of meeting Dr. Tanner in person. So I was surprised and honored to see that the *DWP* program was included in her 2013 obituary:

> Tanner – Laurel N. Dr., a renowned education expert who was awarded the 2007 Lifetime Achievement Award from the Curriculum Studies division of the American Educational Research Association, died on Sunday in Seattle, Washington. She was 84. Dr. Tanner served as a Professor of Curriculum and Instruction and the Director of Urban Education at Temple University in Philadelphia, and served as a professor at the University of Houston. Her 1978 book "Classroom Discipline" led to the development of the *Discipline with Purpose* program, a nationally acclaimed program currently taught in hundreds of schools (*New York Times*, Oct. 25, 2013).

What Is *Discipline with Purpose?*

Discipline with Purpose is a developmental approach used to teach self-discipline to children in kindergarten through ninth grade. Self-discipline is a person's ability to wait and think before acting. We identified 15 natural opportunities to practice self-discipline in everyday life, so natural they can be overlooked. The self-discipline program teaches students to respond in and outside of the classroom by focusing on the opportunities to perform the wait and think before acting behavior.

We divided the 15 skills into three distinct developmental groups using Dr. Tanner's labels: Basic, Constructive and Generative.

The Basic Skills

The Basic Skills are five skills critical for school learning. They are also useful for people in groups, communities, and society. Children from birth until the developmental age of five, are usually coached and cued by adults to learn these skills. The optimum time to intentionally teach and practice these skills is from kindergarten through third grade. Adults often expect children to be able to demonstrate these skills without training. The five Basic Skills are:

1. Listening
2. Following Instructions
3. Asking Questions
4. Sharing: Time, Space, People, Things
5. Interacting Socially

The Constructive Skills

Skills six to ten build on the Basic Skills and, in most cases, are more complex than the first five skills. For example, the skill of sharing taught to primary children now shifts to the skill of cooperation for middle grade students. The skill of following instructions shifts to the more complex skill of independently accomplishing tasks. Learners in grades three to six are at the optimum age to understand the points of view of others and receive instruction on ways to demonstrate each skill. The Constructive Skills focus on developing "children who are contributors to the social good of the classroom rather than beings who simply abide by the rules" (Tanner, 32). The five Constructive Skills are:

1. Cooperating
2. Understanding the Reasons for Rules
3. Independently Accomplishing Tasks
4. Exhibiting Leadership
5. Communicating Effectively

The Generative Skills

Skills 11 to 15, the Generative Skills, are needed when an individual or group is ready to take the initiative to improve groups and society. Learners in sixth grade through high school will struggle to master these skills. The learner must show proficiency in performing and choosing to practice the skill without reminders or coaching. The five Generative Skills are:

1. Organizing: Time, Space, People, Things
2. Resolving Problems
3. Initiating Solutions
4. Distinguishing Facts from Feelings
5. Sacrificing or Serving Others

These 15 natural opportunities, to *wait and think before acting,* form the heart of the *Discipline with Purpose* program. When self-discipline is taught, specific information about each skill is learned, children practice all or part of the skill and they self-evaluate their progress. Since the identification of these skills in 1984, it is now possible for individuals to measure their growth in acquiring self-discipline.

How *Discipline with Purpose* Grew

As the program developed, Paula and I conducted evening classes at educational service units. Creighton University in Omaha, NE sponsored three to five-day workshops each summer. Participants came from all over the U.S., having heard about the program in national conferences, published articles, and through word of mouth. *DWP* presenters traveled to conduct on-site workshops throughout the school year. Six-page newsletters were sent to *DWP* schools eight times a year to share ideas teachers had implemented (today, social media keeps schools connected). Individual schools formed *DWP* Committees charged with setting goals for program implementation. Attendees to training sessions received a list of assumptions during the first hour of the activities and were invited to ask questions to clarify the intent and purpose of the workshop.

There were ten basic assumptions:

1. Cultures flourish when persons have a commitment to work, the willingness and ability to relate to others in a cooperative manner, and have acquired self-discipline.
2. There is a need for adults and youth today to renew their understanding of what it means to be self-disciplined.
3. Self-discipline is a person's ability to *wait and think before acting*. *Discipline with Purpose* has identified 15 natural opportunities in daily life where that pattern is operative.
4. If the skills are unnamed, adults can miss significant opportunities to teach self-discipline to children.
5. When individuals agree on the behaviors expected of self-disciplined persons, they establish a framework for making decisions and resolving conflicts.
6. Acknowledgment of the consequences of one's actions and the willingness to change unhealthy behaviors are necessary components in any cooperative adventure.
7. When skills, instead of personality traits, are used as the standard for evaluating behaviors, confrontation brings about constructive change.
8. Misbehavior can be viewed as a teachable moment, a time to talk about missing skills. Skill talk is neutral talk. It does not demean or put-down another person.
9. The measure of effective leaders in any organization is directly related to the self-discipline skills they have integrated.
10. When individuals demonstrate self-discipline skills collectively, society can be transformed in a positive way.

The initial excitement for the program was from persons who recognized that behaviors categorized as discipline problems were often due to a lack of one or more of the self-discipline skills. Listed below are typical behaviors teachers identified as a disciplinary concern. The problems on the left are directly influenced by a lack of the skill, named on the right, that could alter the problematic behavior.

- Inability to focus and/or clear distractions – Listening
- Starting a project and forgetting what to do – Following Instructions
- Asking the same or similar questions – Asking Questions
- Invading the space of others/leaving classrooms disorderly – Sharing Space

- Bullying – Exhibiting Social Skills
- Inability to function well in a group – Cooperating
- Pitting one adult against another – Understanding Reasons for Rules
- Inability to set realistic goals – Independently Accomplishing Tasks
- Inability to resist peer pressure – Exhibiting Leadership
- Using poor nonverbal or verbal skills – Communicating Effectively
- Inability to organize time, space, things, or relationships – Organizing
- Arguing when corrected - Resolving Problems
- Unable to take the initiative to resolve problems – Initiating Solutions to Problems
- Easily angered – Distinguishing Facts from Feelings
- Engaging in self-centered behaviors – Sacrificing/Serving Others

When children fiddled or could not clear away distractions, we taught teachers to respond by teaching the steps of listening, rather than viewing this behavior as a discipline problem (see chapter 4). When learners did not complete homework or classwork, they were assigned a time to complete the work. In addition, we evaluated the ability to follow a set of written instructions and provided strategies to independently complete tasks (see chapters 5 and 12). When students couldn't function well in a group, we addressed the skills of cooperation and social etiquette (See chapters 8 and 10).

Once students knew classroom expectations and learned how to practice and achieve the self-discipline skills, teachers reported a reduction in out-of-bounds behavior. Students were more willing to accept criticism and self-correct. Teachers learned to distinguish when to use discipline or promote skill training accordingly. They also learned to distinguish between a motivational problem and a discipline problem and understood how to handle these differently. Using the 15 self-discipline skills, adults had a framework that provided direction and purpose for children growing up. Teachers, parents, and students became co-partners in learning and practicing the skills. The result was a more civil classroom environment.

Because of *Discipline with Purpose*, thousands of educators in the United States are devoted to building and maintaining a school culture where students, teachers, and parents clearly understand the goals of discipline and self-discipline. School staffs have developed three to five-year continuous improvement plans as they work to integrate the 15 self-discipline skills. An online three-hour graduate credit course is offered each March through May at a Midwest state college. Teachers ministering to teachers have created and field-tested over 270 age-appropriate lesson plans that focus on the skills.

Teaching the 15 Skills

There are four ways to teach the 15 skills. With each process used, there is an observable by-product. The four teaching methods include:

Modeling – Adults demonstrate by their actions that they know and choose to use the 15 self-discipline skills. The by-product is positive, self-assured adults who confidently teach skills whenever they observe they are lacking. Adults have developed their own code outlining specific ways they will consistently model the skills. (See Chapter 18: A Skill Code Saves the Day)

Pre-teaching – Adults and children plan how to have an enjoyable time when engaging in an activity. The *who, what, when, why,* and *how* questions are asked, so everyone is clear on the expected skills they'll need to demonstrate. The by-product comprises checklists, step-by-step outlines, and T-charts used to pre-teach, evaluate, and review each time the same activity is planned (See Chapters 5 and 16).

Infusion – Adults intentionally highlight the skills when teaching, interacting with others, or planning activities. Illustrations of the skills are visible. The by-product is a common vocabulary used by parents and teachers. Students know and understand how the skills look and sound in action.

Using the *DWP* Curriculum – Model lessons to teach a skill are used once every three to four weeks before children are invited to practice all or part of the skill. The by-product is a student's self-assessment of their personal growth/progress in mastering the featured skill.

All the skills come into play during each phase of a child's development; thus, they need not be sequentially taught. Focusing on four skills at the beginning of the school year can help establish a classroom where learning will take place. These four skills include listening, following instructions, understanding the rules, and resolving problems when rules are not followed. These skills are further explained in chapters three, four, five, eleven and seventeen. In a less formal way, parents can focus on these same skills as they teach the skill of listening and give guidance when children are asked to follow instructions. Chapter 11 suggests three home rules and Chapter 17 contains productive vocabulary to use when problem solving.

In school, teachers focus on the skills students are lacking. If five or more students exhibit the same unproductive behaviors, teachers know it is time to provide information and practice regarding the missing skill (refer to Marti's story at the beginning of Chapter 4).

The Basic, Constructive, and Generative skills can be used as a guide for determining the skill vocabulary that will best suit a student or students. An example of how a mother switched her vocabulary as she comforted her 12-year-old son can be found in Chapter 13.

Reasons for Writing *Discipline with Purpose: Nurturing a Child's Self-Discipline*

Children are born with cognitive strengths and/or challenges. Some excel naturally, while others lack important executive functions. All children can attain a level of self-discipline when adults intentionally nurture that development and value them just the way they are. Our words and actions can convey confidence in their abilities to handle life situations. We nurture children when we teach skills they will need to fulfill their unique vocations. All children can learn to feel safe when restraint, respect, and consideration for others are primary goals.

Recently, I came across *110 Rules of Civility and Decent Behavior* that George Washington copied in his handwriting book when he was about 16. The 16th century precepts compiled by Jesuit instructors helped shape young students into men. The pointers included instructions on living respectfully, caring for mind, body, and attitude, courtesy toward superiors, table manners, and conversation tips. I was struck by the attention given to everyday activities. Learning how to perform these activities in a civilized manner was considered important to teach. Using the precepts as a guide helped to define a gentleman ready to move freely in all types of societies.

Similarly, the 15 self-discipline skills outlined in this book can become the modern-day precepts to guide youth to be responsible and help shape personalities. It doesn't matter what grade you teach. It doesn't matter if you teach math, computer science, study skills, debate, reading, or culinary arts. Every person who accepts the title "teacher" could be teaching self-discipline. It doesn't matter if you are in a nuclear family, stepfamily, single-parent family, or extended family. Communities of respect form when members understand the nature and purpose of self-discipline and practice the skills that foster its growth. As Paul Forni wrote in his book *Choosing Civility*, "Being civil means being constantly aware of others and weaving restraint, respect, and consideration into the very fabric of this awareness. The heart of being civil requires people to be self-controlled and exhibit restraint" (2002, p. 9).

How This Book is Organized

It is my intent that readers begin this book with an overview of this practical method of teaching self-discipline. Here is a summary of chapter content:

- In Chapter 1, the reader will find a distinction between discipline and punishment and an explanation of foundational components for developing self-discipline.
- In Chapter 2, the definition of self-discipline is expanded upon along with an explanation of how the skills within the 15-skills framework are connected.
- Chapter 3 provides background information on the Basic skills and suggests motivational ways to help children practice the skills.
- Chapters 4 through 8 feature each of the five Basic skills. Each skill chapter ends with a story that illustrates the skill vocabulary adults use to nurture, coach, model and encourage skill practice.
- Chapter 9 includes insights for teaching the Constructive Skills.
- Chapters 10 through 14 provide an explanation of each of the five Constructive Skills.
- Chapter 15 offers insights into why the Generative Skills are difficult for children in grades six through eight to master and addresses the role of the adult during this time.

- Chapters 16 through 20 provide an explanation of each of the five Generative Skills.
- Chapter 21 is a quick reference of 60 suggestions adults can use when teaching self-discipline. These action steps provide adults with an opportunity to evaluate how well or poorly children are able to practice the skills without prompts or cues. They also provide training for adults who want to monitor their own understanding and practice of self-discipline.

In the years since *Discipline with Purpose* began, we've collected insights and anecdotes from practitioners, which are included in this book. Some stories and lived experiences might sound too good to be true, but true they are. Teaching children with respect while teaching them how to develop themselves has powerful results.

An effective way to summarize *Discipline with Purpose* is to consider what it is not. *DWP* is a process used by adults and children; it is not a program used to control children. Its techniques teach self-discipline; it is not a program to teach compliance. It recognizes developmental changes; strategies change with the age of the child. The program does not claim one right way of doing things. Strategies focus on appropriate behaviors rather than misbehavior.

DWP treats skills as skills; it does not treat skills as rules. Skills cannot be broken! The program challenges adults to view misbehavior as a teachable moment; it does not view giving a consequence as the only response to misbehavior. Children learn and practice skills using their unique learning styles; they do not learn skills using a standard cognitive step-by-step approach. Adults learn to use skill language to empower students and avoid criticism or negativity that can antagonize. *DWP* promotes productive behaviors over a long period of time; it is not a quick fix.

CHAPTER 1

The Foundation of Self-Discipline

The Parent's Responsibility

It is no accident that the words 'disciple' and 'discipline' are spelled alike. Both come from two Latin root words: "discipulus," which means a disciple, and "discere" or "disco," which means to learn. A disciple imitates both the life and the teaching of a master. Parents, as the first educators of their children, model behavior and enculturate children into family values and expectations. Parents can unintentionally model inappropriate behavior and/or intentionally verbalize the what and why of their modeling. This modeling becomes imminently important as parents ready a child to self-regulate and choose appropriate behavior when adults cannot be present.

Discipline leading to self-discipline begins at the birth of a child. Informed parents know a baby will be completely dependent upon them for basic needs. A parent's time will be dictated by these needs. Much physical, emotional, moral, intellectual, and social development takes place in the first five years of a child's life and is the foundation for self-discipline.

The *Discipline with Purpose (DWP)* program has been developed on the premise that becoming self-disciplined begins at birth. Proponents of the program believe self-discipline begins when parents instruct children in the most loving ways to understand they are not the center of the universe, that there is a will stronger than their own worth listening to. A child's temperament, innate needs, the environment, and parental capabilities will factor into the ease or difficulty of achieving these goals. There are a variety of discipline strategies parents can use:

- Assess a child's behavior before acting.
- Attend to the child's basic needs even if their own activities are interrupted.
- Be consistent in actions.
- Act quickly when a child's actions are dangerous, abusive, or irrational.

- Give encouragement and focus on positive behaviors.
- Set routines so children get rest, eat at scheduled times, and have a balance between attention from adults and alone time.
- Help a child learn to read body language by using facial expressions and a voice tone that communicates disapproval or displeasure.
- Call a child by name and wait until he/she looks at you before making a request.
- Be specific. Don't say, "Get ready to go," but, "Please put on your coat." Say it firmly, but in a friendly, calm, and unhurried manner.
- Word requests as statements, not questions. The obvious answer to "Would you like to pick up your toys?" is "No."
- Look at the child when talking and require the child to repeat what he heard.
- Repeat instructions rather than change the instructions.
- Tell children what they *should do* rather than what they *should not do.* Show the child *how* to do something.
- Avoid making idle threats or idle promises.

Parental modeling, coaching, and cueing of social behaviors is an ongoing task.

The Teacher's Responsibility

When children enter school, teachers will build on what the parents have accomplished in home discipline (see kindergarten readiness in the appendix). Kindergarten teachers identify the children who are ready to move from adult-imposed discipline to self-discipline. These children comply with teacher requests and can function well in a group. They have developed socially acceptable habits and behavior patterns. In short, there has been structure, nurture, and discipline in their early lives. Kindergarten teachers recognize children who attempt to have their needs met at the expense of others, and those who need remedial help to facilitate learning. The task of disciplining children will go hand-in-hand with teaching self-discipline.

Children with Delayed Capabilities

Infants born prematurely or children with delayed cognitive impairment can have undeveloped capabilities, including the ability to pay attention, organize and plan work, initiate tasks, stay focused, regulate emotions, and self-monitor. All of these capabilities are essential in developing self-discipline. Children with delayed capabilities are held accountable for learning self-discipline but acquiring the skills may take longer and may require more patience from the adult. Creating a caring and nurturing environment in the classroom is essential. Adults can establish routines, model social behavior, teach students self-talk, and create and maintain a supportive relationship with children. Coping mechanisms to assist both adults and children are described throughout this book.

Five Times Disciplinary Action is Needed

Disciplinary action means making the first move to remedy misbehaviors. This action can be as simple as asking a question, investigating the situation, or getting the child's point of view. How one responds will be determined by the severity of the misbehavior. Adults can confidently take disciplinary action in the following situations:

- From birth to age 5 when parents are teaching children in a loving way there is a will stronger than their own and they are not the center of the universe.
- When someone is in physical or psychological danger or puts others in danger (e.g. using normal objects in dangerous ways, striking out, put-downs).
- When someone is abusive in tone or gesture (e.g. shouting, screaming, using abusive language, bullying, or harassment).
- When someone is out of control or has pushed beyond the limits of reasonable action (e.g. tantrums, overly tired, basic needs not met, continue to exhibit socially unacceptable behavior after correction).
- When all possible means of helping a child have failed, help is required from another professional. In these cases, teachers need to document all attempts that have failed to redirect and teach appropriate behaviors.

Police or Teach

Adults can respond to a child's poor choice in two ways –
they can police or teach. How one responds depends on perception
of the child's action. If the child's action indicates a developmental
lack of skill, adults have a wonderful opportunity to teach the
missing skill. A dangerous, disrespectful, or disruptive behavior will
require disciplinary action first, followed by attempts to teach an
alternative behavior. Is the unacceptable behavior due to a discipline
issue or a lack of motivation? Discipline problems typically require
preventative strategies as well as short-term interventions.
Motivational problems require long-term, individualized
interventions.

A recent cartoon portrays two students sitting on a bench
outside the principal's office waiting to be disciplined. "What did
you do?" asks the first child.

"I forgot my homework," the other says. "What did you do?"

"I blew up the science experiment."

In this situation, an astute administrator would recognize the
differences between these two offenses. She may choose to have the
first child practice the self-discipline skills of following instructions
and completing tasks independently. The principal would need to
discern if the student had learned these self-discipline skills but chose
not to use them. This would result in a consequence that will help
the student to complete homework. Disciplinary action for the
second student includes immediate adult intervention to provide
school safety and consequences for failing to follow a rule. To
provide additional help, the principal would need to discern if the
student blew up the science project intentionally or if another motive
prompted the action.

Discipline Versus Punishment

Discipline strives to replace an unwanted behavior with a
desirable one. Punishment can eliminate a negative behavior but fail
to replace it with a productive behavior. The purpose of discipline is
to teach an alternative way of behaving. Good discipline takes time

18

and energy; consequences should be logical and encourage restitution. However, punishment can inflict harm in the name of good and may not allow children to make up for bad behaviors. Punishment that does not allow restitution fails to teach civility or self-discipline. *Discipline with Purpose* defines discipline as rules and regulations that govern the conduct of adults and children to allow for effective interaction, so that learning can take place. *Merriam-Webster.com*, an online dictionary, defines punishment as "a penalty inflicted on an offender," that can cause, "suffering, pain, or loss that serves as retribution."

School discipline and parental discipline are viewed differently. As primary teachers, parents are protective of their ability to discipline their own children in the manner they see fit. Some parents find it culturally acceptable and even preferable for a teacher to give a child a few swats rather than a school suspension. The American Academy of Pediatrics (AAP) defines spanking as, "non-injurious, openhanded hitting with the intention of modifying child behavior" (2018, p. 1). The AAP has advised parents against the use of spanking and nonphysical punishment that humiliates, scares, or threatens the child.

Teachers have little control over the type of discipline children receive before coming to school. Consequently, it is important for educators to inform parents of the type of discipline that will be part of the school environment. The school handbook lists consequences a student will incur for exhibiting unsafe, illegal, or immoral actions. Most teachers will have a classroom management plan that will outline the steps a child can take to self-correct before an adult will intervene (see Chapter 17).

In one sense, a child will perceive any action that inconveniences him or her as punishment. If a five-year-old is confined to sit in time-out for three minutes, this *wait* period can seem like punishment. Likewise, if an adult takes a cell phone away from a young teen for a few days, the teen is likely to believe the action is unfair. Effective discipline involves understanding how to treat a child in different stages of development. A clear relationship between behavior and consequences is important in administering discipline. Central to establishing effective consequences will be a trusting relationship between teacher and child and a loving relationship between parent and child.

Perhaps the greatest learning experiences have been the times we made mistakes as children, and instead of punishing us, the adults helped us correct the things we did wrong. Children are in process, still growing; therefore, the posture adults should take toward children who make bad judgments can be one of helpfulness. We can explore together what went wrong. We can work together to correct wrongs. We can strategize for the next time. Effective discipline requires that both the adult and the child's self-esteems remain intact after a discussion or confrontation. Teaching obedience, conformity, and good manners is not enough if children are to become socially responsible. Social responsibility includes being sensitive to the needs and problems of others.

Similarities between Discipline and Self-Discipline

In Chapter Two, we focus on the difference between disciplining a child and teaching self-discipline, though these two concepts have much in common. Effective discipline and teaching self-discipline are both designed to teach acceptable social standards. They both build character and personality traits such as honesty, integrity, and resiliency. They can help form a conscience, teaching children how to make personal decisions for the good of the self and others.

> "We now live in an age of idolatry of the Self. We have persuaded ourselves that first and foremost we live to realize our own Selves for our own good. Having made the Self the central concern and value in our lives, we should not be surprised if self-centered behaviors have become more prevalent than altruistic ones. We shouldn't be surprised if civility has suffered. The more we focus on ourselves and our self-gratification the less moral energy we have available to spend on others and the less attuned we are to others' wellbeing... What many of us are learning or relearning now is the essential role that self-control plays in the lives of democracies."
>
> Choosing Civility, P.M. Forni, p. 169

CHAPTER 2

What Is Self-Discipline?

Upon hearing the word self-discipline for the first time, one second grader remarked, "That sounds like it would hurt!" This comment illustrates the perception that acquiring self-discipline can cause discomfort or require monumental motivation.

The dictionary describes self-discipline in the following ways: 1) the "ability to make yourself do things that should be done;" 2) the ability "to control one's feelings and overcome weaknesses;" and, "the ability to pursue what one thinks is right despite temptations to abandon it" (Dictionary.com). These descriptors indicate that effort and restraint are needed to acquire self-discipline.

To find a simplified description of self-discipline to begin instructing children five years of age, as Dr. Tanner suggested, Paula and I conducted an unscientific survey. We asked adults, "What evidence do you have that you are a self-disciplined person?" Without having knowledge of the 15 skills framework adults described isolated behaviors.

The skill that helped them acquire these behaviors are indicated in parentheses.

- I get up every morning. Have been doing this for years. This must show I am self-disciplined. (Organization of time)
- I can stick to a diet or project when I put my mind to it. (Initiates solutions to problems)
- I'm a good listener. (Listening)
- I get to appointments on time. (Organization of time)
- I'm a self-starter. No one needs to tell me what to do. (Accomplishes tasks independently)
- I know what's right and I follow the rules of society. (Understands rules)
- Not sure what I do, but people tell me I'm very disciplined.

Adults who did not consider themselves to be self-disciplined answered in the following ways:

- I never get things done that I plan to do. (Organization of time, things)
- I can't make myself do what I don't feel like doing. (Distinguishing fact from feeling)
- I can't stick to diets. (Initiating solutions to problems, Accomplishing tasks independently)
- I'm not consistent in what I do. I'm ruled by my emotions. (Distinguishing fact from feeling)
- I never had much discipline in my life as I was growing up. I've always done just what I wanted to do. (Distinguishing facts from feelings)
- I'm not sure what self-discipline is. Everyone has a different idea of what it means to be self-disciplined.

Self-discipline Defined – WAIT, THINK, ACT

It is difficult to measure growth using a norm or standard when everyone has a different idea of what it means to be self-disciplined. Since self-discipline requires restraint, the most basic ingredient is the ability to *wait*. While waiting, a person *thinks* about how to *act*. *Waiting* is the skill that helps people delay impulsive behavior. Five-year-olds can understand what it means to 'WAIT' and are thus able to begin intentionally practicing self-discipline. Character, virtue, respect, charitable works, moral actions, and self-esteem are all by-products of self-discipline.

The need to wait is deeply ingrained in our everyday lives. Yet modern society often avoids it. We impatiently honk car horns at traffic jams. We search for the shortest lines in check-out counters. For our aches or pains, we rush to painkillers that will hurry away what ails us, rather than tend to long-term remedies requiring healthier habits. We look for programs and practices that have a quick fix. Our technological age has encouraged us to speed up our thoughts rather than reflect upon them.

There are 15 natural opportunities in daily life where people can practice *waiting, thinking,* and *acting*. Adults and children can identify opportunities for *waiting*, when they understand that the heart of self-discipline is to pause before acting. The skills that require the use of the *wait, think, act* pattern are not acquired solely through maturation, though some people seem to have an innate ability to pause. This central pattern of self-discipline can be intentionally taught and observed; skills specifically defined can be measured.

The 15 Skills Framework

To make the concept of self-discipline concrete for students, we created simple illustrations. The illustrations pictured are the original set created in 1984. Information regarding updated versions can be found in the references section under "Develop Education Skills."

The illustrations used in subsequent chapters were designed by the late Ginni Engelbrecht, an artist and nature lover. Teachers using *DWP*, crafted illustrations of the skills that fit their subjects and reflected the cultures of their students. Such illustrations exist for Native American, Hispanic, and African-American sub-cultures. Specialists have created skill posters to use in physical education, art, technology, and music classes. There is a set of pictures reflecting Christian scriptures, and even a set of illustrations that indicate how the 15 skills are needed when golfing.

Companion Skills

The color-coded framework shows how the skills are related, overlap, and build upon one another:

Green: Listening, Cooperating, Resolving Problems

Black: Following Instructions, Completing Tasks Independently, Organizing

Red: Asking Questions, Understanding Reasons for Rules, Initiating Solutions

Yellow: Sharing, Communicating, Distinguishing Facts from Feelings

Blue: Exhibiting Social Skills and Leadership, Sacrificing/Serving Others.

Basic K-3rd	Constructive 3-6th	Generative 6-10th
LISTENING	COOPERATION	ORGANIZATION
FOLLOWING INSTRUCTIONS	REASONS FOR RULES	RESOLVING PROBLEMS
ASKING QUESTIONS	COMPLETING A TASK	INITIATING SOLUTIONS
SHARING	LEADERSHIP	FACT VS. FEELING
SOCIAL SKILLS	COMMUNICATION	SERVICE-OTHERS

Teachers have used the 15-skills framework to predict skill strengths and weaknesses. They have noticed that the children who question everything when they are in the primary grades are likely to challenge the rules when they are in middle school. By junior high and high school, these pre-teens can initiate solutions to problems and offer suggestions and opinions on a variety of topics (these are the skills outlined in red in the skills framework).

The child in middle school who has difficulty organizing, might not have been given opportunities to independently accomplish tasks or may struggle to follow instructions. This happens sometimes when adults rescue children, thus not giving them an opportunity to figure things out on their own.

Remedial instruction in the skills of following instructions and independently accomplish tasks will help the child gain the ability to organize (these three skills are outlined in black in the skills framework).

Keep the 15-Skills Framework Together

When consulting the framework, adults sometimes insist that children demonstrate the Basic Skills of listening and following instructions before challenging/coaching/allowing students to practice leadership, problem solving, or other advanced skills. This mistaken idea does not recognize that skills are developmental, not sequential.

Consequently, adults sacrifice the power of the entire 15-skills framework as a teaching tool and motivator. The adult who believes listening and following instructions must be mastered before higher level skills, is likely to remain in the role of a disciplinarian. They will continue to emphasize the need for children to be compliant, rather than self-disciplined.

> Basic discipline is important, and many teachers would wish for no more. 'If they could only listen and follow directions,' are words on the lips of thousands of teachers. But being able to listen and follow directions is not the end of discipline. These competencies are turning points and not end points. Basic [skills] must be just the beginning in a democratic society (Tanner 1978, p. 32).

Children with learning difficulties may need to develop coping mechanisms to demonstrate the skills of listening and following instructions. However, these children may readily share and make sacrifices. Gifted students who are good communicators often struggle with the skill of cooperation. These learners might find it difficult to work with others but can complete work independently. When the entire framework is used as a teaching tool, adults can validate advanced skill strengths.

Identifying skill strengths and weaknesses is also needed for adults. An educator may be a terrific organizer and create well-developed lessons but might not be able to listen and distinguish facts from feelings. Consequently, students might not become engaged in class activities. There is value for adults to admit to children that we continue to practice the skills.

Some aspect of each skill is taught at all grade levels using developmentally appropriate strategies. The elements of a skill will move from simple to increasingly complex. When the skill of distinguishing facts from feelings, a Generative Skill, is taught in second grade, children learn to name feelings and describe where their bodies feel each emotion. They learn to read a person's face and body language.

Students in the middle grades experience mixed emotions. They will find it difficult to describe one feeling and embarrassing to name where the feeling is in the body. Dealing with mixed emotions means refraining from acting until you can sort feelings from facts. It includes being able to verbalize why mixed emotions might cause inaction. These are the concepts older students learn about the skill of distinguishing facts from feelings.

Why Talk about Self-Discipline as Skills?

Like any other skill, self-discipline is acquired through practice. Each person will use their unique learning style to acquire the skill. For example, when learning the skill of following instructions, teachers can guide students to use one of the following methods:

- Some people learn to follow instructions when they can read, write, listen to a speaker and think about a list of steps. They privately think through the steps and when they feel internally ready, they begin the task.

- Some people need a buddy or partner to role model the skill. They ask questions and check to make sure they are doing things correctly. Once shown how to perform a skill, they imitate the steps and make the skill their own.

- Some people use the trial and error method. They are likely to begin work before instructions are provided. Through coaching and correction, they adjust until they complete the task. They can also lose interest and settle for a less-than-complete project if correction is too harsh or too constant. With humor and a person they trust, they will accept correction and continue to practice the skill.

Implications for Teachers

When teachers observe the behaviors of children in terms of the self-discipline skills, they realize how often adults discipline children for behaviors that indicate a lack of one of the first five self-discipline skills. Here are some examples:

- Every day the teacher next to me sends students into the hallway for various reasons. Most of the reasons stem from the fact the students are lacking one or more of the first five skills. Sending students into the hallway and not teaching them about the missing skill is ineffective. The students are growing more defiant and taking on an "I don't care" attitude.

- In our school, teachers prefer a variety of teaching styles. If a class of students is walking down the hallway and talking, Teacher A might say, "Bill, we're in the hall so lips are zipped and our hands are at our sides. May I please have your cooperation?" Teacher B might say, "Bill, you're staying in at recess for every minute you continue to talk and not follow directions." In the first example the teacher recognizes that sharing space is a skill. In the second, the behavior is treated as a discipline issue.

- I noticed that the first couple of weeks, teachers spent a lot of time teaching and modeling the first five skills. After that, we expected students to know and display the skills. Instead of mentoring and coaching the reluctant student, consequences were levied.

- A few teachers give each student three chips at the start of class. Each time a skill is not followed, the teacher nonchalantly grabs a chip from the student's desk. In this way, the teacher can continue the lesson without interrupting the rest of the class. At the end of the day each student marks the number of chips they have left in their notebook. Students don't receive feedback about why a chip is taken away. I wonder if a child changes their behavior out of fear or because they understand the missing self-discipline skill. I wonder if the teacher is turning skills into rules.

As the skills are taught, modeled, and infused into existing curriculum, a shift is made from disciplinarian to teacher of self-discipline. Adults who understand the skills and have memorized their placement in the skill framework, can use developmentally appropriate skill language with children of all ages. This allows adults to focus on civility in ordinary daily actions.

Implications for Parents

Parents report that understanding the Basic, Constructive and Generative skills has helped them become realistic about the behaviors they expect children to demonstrate without prompts. They learn to teach children that 'growing up' has less to do with age and more to do with acquiring and demonstrating the skills of self-discipline.

When parents decide to teach self-discipline, they make an intentional decision to avoid the following pitfalls:

Inconsistency: Saying one thing but doing another. Children learn not to trust our words or they learn if they wait long enough, the strong stance we took on the issue will dissolve.

Shouting: Raising our voices only demonstrates that *we* have not mastered the higher-level self-discipline skills. It shows that we cannot separate fact from feeling and resolve problems in a rational manner.

Idle threats: While idle threats might provide some relief, they do little to change inappropriate behaviors.

Negative power-plays: One person cannot come out the winner, and another the loser if we want to develop people with high self-esteem.

No follow-through: Sometimes an initial correction is not discussed again. Checking in with a child after a confrontation suggests that, as adults, we understand how difficult it can be to learn a new skill.

Thinking the worst: Nothing comes from nothing. Failing to wait until our own attitudes are positive before correcting behavior might seem more like retaliation rather than teaching.

After listening to a presentation of the 15-skills, a father shared that when his first son was born, he made a list of all the qualities he wanted to teach. He kept the list in his pocket. He realized almost every one of the skills was represented in his list. "Talking about the qualities as skills makes my task of teaching them concrete and more useful," he said.

Implications for Students

The self-discipline framework of 15 skills has helped students to:

Identify the skills they have mastered and acknowledge their assets. "I used to get in trouble in a more physical sense... Now we do a lot more 'talking it out.' I like it and my parents do too" (Adam, Grade 8).

Identify the skills they need to practice and set realistic goals for mastery. "It is a challenge to see if we can live up to the 15 *DWP* skills" (student, Grade 8).

More readily accept compliments from adults, because they understand the work that goes into acquiring a skill. "These skills help us deal with problems with our friends, our families, and even ourselves" (Kristi, Grade 8).

Become conscious of the choices they make that help or hinder a community. "*DWP* teaches us to show respect to others and respect for ourselves" (Cassie, Grade 8).

Challenge themselves to use their skills to change conditions that are unjust or harmful to others. "This program has taught us that the reward for proper behavior is in yourself. It becomes a part of you" (Jacob, Grade 9).

Learn that performing a skill because of a prompt from an adult is different from acquiring the skill and choosing to use it on their own. "We are learning skills so we'll know how to act when we are pressured by our peers. I feel stronger in handling myself" (Jason, Grade 8).

Review Chapters 1 & 2

1. Discipline is defined as a _____ of rules and regulations that govern the conduct of the _____ and the _____ to allow for effective interaction, so that _____ can take place.
2. Self-discipline is a person's ability to WAIT, _____, and ACT.
3. There are _____ self-discipline skills identified in Discipline with Purpose.
4. The first five skills are called Basic and include the skills of _____, Following Instructions, _____, Sharing and Exhibiting Social Skills.
5. The _____ Skills include Cooperating, Understanding the Reasons for Rules, _____ Leadership, and _____.
6. The _____Skills include the ability to _____, Resolve Problems, Initiate Solutions, Distinguish _____from _____ and Serve Others.
7. In a loving manner parents can teach children from birth until the developmental age of five that there is a _____ stronger than their own worth listening to and that they are not the _____ of the universe.
8. Adults can confidently take a leadership role and discipline whenever there is danger, _____, and _____.
9. Skills cannot be broken. They are not the same as _____.
10. It takes _____ to view misbehavior as a teachable moment.

Word Bank

Constructive	System	Will	Rules	Listening
Generative	Center	15	THINK	Adult
Organize	Disrespect	Skill	Feelings	Disruption
Communication	Facts	Child	Learning	Asking Questions
Independently Complete Tasks				

CHAPTER 3

Teaching the Basic Skills

```
                        BASIC SKILLS
Coached:  Birth-Pre-school
Optimum time to teach: Kindergarten – Third Grade

    1.  Listening
    2.  Following Instructions
    3.  Asking Questions
    4.  Sharing Time, Space, People, Things
    5.  Interacting Socially
```

To teach self-discipline, as with other subjects, the educator learns specific content for skill practice. There is a formal and an informal curriculum. This chapter suggests ways to motivate primary students to practice the first five skills and addresses issues related to teaching the Basic Skills to older students. Basic Skills are the skills critical for school learning.

Children from birth until the developmental age of five can be coached by adults to learn these skills, but often are not. The optimum time to intentionally teach these skills is from kindergarten through third grade. Children with challenges in learning may be delayed in developing these skills.

Internal Motivation

One goal of teaching self-discipline is to develop a child's desire to demonstrate the skills, finding them helpful in achieving success. Adults hint at this when they tell students to "work toward your goal, improve yourself, gain the satisfaction of knowing you did your best." But encouraging phrases or pep talks can be abstract and ineffective if students do not have a clear understanding of the skills of self-discipline. Children need concrete ways to think about abstract concepts. To motivate young children, we refer to the self-discipline skills as hidden skills, hidden powers, or hidden gifts. Each teacher can use the term that best suits students.

One way to introduce the concept of self-discipline is by creating a bulletin board with a heading such as "Our Hidden Powers." Illustrations of the five Basic Skills are placed on the board face down with a large question mark on the back of each illustration. The teacher makes no mention of the board until at least one child notices and asks about it. The teacher tells the class to *wait and think* about what the phrase means. Successful teachers in the *Discipline with Purpose* program look for opportunities to help children practice the *wait, think, act* pattern.

Strategies

Instruction often begins by focusing on the title "Our Hidden Powers." Children learn that everyone has hidden powers or skills; they are inside of you, in your head and heart, hands, and feet. They are hidden because no one knows you have the skills unless you decide to show them in your actions. The best time to show a hidden power is when no one reminds you to do so. Whenever you choose to show your hidden skills, there will be a benefit to you and the people around you.

Upon hearing this information, a young boy raised his hand and said, "I don't have any hidden powers." The teacher replied, "Oh, but you do. In fact, you are using a high-level power right now. It is even higher than the five you will learn about here." She was referring to the fact that the young boy was able to communicate his thoughts. Communication is a Constructive Skill and one that primary students will learn but are not expected to master.

As the lesson continues, the students speculate on what might be behind each question-marked poster. Each student receives a small six-by-four-inch, 20-page blank booklet made of card stock and held together with metal rings. The children personalize their booklet covers by printing the words "Hidden Powers" or "Hidden Skills" and illustrating what those words could mean. One child might draw a star, another, five balloons and the sun. In one case, a young man with learning difficulties started at the back of his book, but his message was clear. He drew a person's rib cage with three bones on each side and a red heart in the middle with the words "bump, bump, bump."

The next time the concept of hidden powers is discussed, the teacher displays the first skill of listening. Children learn information about the skill and record in their booklets what they want to remember. They make tally marks to track the times they choose to demonstrate the skill. Self-assessment begins when students are actively aware they have chosen to use a skill without a reminder.

Another method used by a *DWP* teacher involves a cut-out boy or girl wearing a cape with the letters SD (Self-Discipline) on the front of their shirt. The name of each student is printed on a cut-out. As students earn a set number of tally marks for demonstrating a skill, their SD kid advances higher on the board. When they reach a goal line, they are awarded a self-discipline laminated license. The license indicates a student intentionally practiced self-discipline.

Music is used to enhance learning. Children learn the song "Be a Self-Disciplined Kid," sung to the tune of "Hickory, Dickory, Dock."

> Be a self-disciplined kid
> And use your hidden power
> Ev'ry day in work and play,
> Be a self-disciplined kid.

Lines one, three, and four repeat as the second line reviews the five Basic Skills.

> Be a self-disciplined kid
> Use Listening skills today (or Follow Instructions today, Ask good questions today, Practice Sharing today, Use Social Skills today.)
> Ev'ry day in work and play,
> Be a self-disciplined kid.

Focusing on one skill for a period of three weeks is a good way to begin training children to practice self-discipline behaviors. Teachers develop experiential activities that encourage skill practice. They assign and encourage children to author stories or poems that highlight skills and provide homework assignments that require students to teach parents about the skills. Adults can weave skill vocabulary into everyday interactions. The following phrases have been helpful as teachers infuse the skill language into daily activities.

- I can see Joseph is using his hidden power of listening. (Listening)
- How many instructions would you like to try to follow? (Following Instructions)
- Ask me *every* question you have about what you heard. (Asking Questions)
- I need a volunteer who wants to practice the skill of sharing today. (Sharing)
- Who will demonstrate their social skills and make our guest feel welcomed? (Social Skills)

Internal motivation grows when adults compliment students for practicing a skill. This is especially true if the skill highlighted is one that is developmentally difficult for a child.

External Motivation

Motivation to perform the skills can be external as well as internal. External motivation in the form of rewards, praise, or privileges can provide an incentive for young people to live up to the expectations of the community. Children with delayed capabilities appreciate external motivators such as:

- Certificates of achievement
- Recognition in a school newspaper
- Pictures of students practicing the skills placed on a bulletin board
- The privilege of representing the school in the community
- The privilege of teaching a skill to another group of students
- Earning a leadership task in the classroom, school, or community
- Postcards or notes sent to parents telling of a student's skill accomplishments.

To help motivate students, teachers can identify shortcomings and help students learn specific skills. When students lack *understanding* – don't know what the teacher expects – teachers are able to use the following interventions:

- Teach simple facts about the skills.
- Help students record or organize the information.
- Discuss examples from daily life when a skill is used.
- Identify students who demonstrate the skill and ask them to give tips to others learning the skill.
- Intentionally teach one or more of the skill lessons contained in *Discipline with Purpose.*

When students lack *ability* to perform a skill, teachers can:

- Role-play the right and wrong ways to practice the skill.
- Let each student set a goal for skill improvement.
- Designate a length of time when students will practice the skill.
- Provide students options to record their progress.
- Evaluate progress and set new goals.

When students lack *motivation* to learn and practice the skills, teachers can self-evaluate by examining their relationship with the student or students.

- How genuine is the care and concern that is being conveyed to the student? Does the teacher role-model the skills?
- How much enthusiasm does the teacher bring to her teaching and how engaged are the students in the lessons?
- Does the teacher have parental support for teaching self-discipline skills to students?
- Are there other factors beyond the teacher's control causing the lack of motivation?

Every person, child, and adult has self-discipline skills, some more highly developed than others. When positive skills are acknowledged in a concrete manner, everyone feels valued and there is incentive for continued practice. This also creates positive relationships that allow correction and suggestions for remedial practice, which children will understand as opportunities for growth rather than criticism. Imagine the consistency developed when children hear the same message in kindergarten through ninth grade about skills of self-discipline. Picture the empowerment and confidence a young child develops through habitually learning productive ways to *wait!*

The Basic Skills Taught to Older Students

Teachers have noticed that the movement from learning the Basic Skills to learning the Constructive Skills begins around January of third grade. When students return to school after the holiday, many will find the terminology "hidden skills" is no longer a motivating factor. By the end of third grade, adults must make a paradigm shift to develop internal and external motivation in different ways (this shift in language and incentives is described in Chapter Nine, when we consider the Constructive Skills).

Many teachers assume by fourth grade children will have mastered the basic self-discipline skills. This will be true for some students. Many will be familiar with skill language and concepts, but it should never be assumed these skills will quickly become part of a student's behavior. If they have never been formally and intentionally taught, children will have neither the reference for self-discipline nor the incentive to demonstrate the skills. It will be important for all teachers to review the Basic Skills in an age appropriate manner at the beginning of each school year, when students tend to watch teachers closely.

Those first few days determine if students will view their teacher primarily as a disciplinarian or as a teacher of self-discipline. What will they be able to learn? Will the teacher know how to establish order in a classroom? Does the teacher have a sense of humor and seem to value each student? Will the teacher require all students to respect their peers and establish a civil classroom? Does the teacher talk about self-discipline in skill language? In the first few days, students determine if the school year will be successful or fraught with difficulties.

Introducing the Concept of Self-Discipline

Working with middle grade and older students, *Discipline with Purpose* teachers begin the year with a discussion of discipline and self-discipline. Students receive a home assignment to think about, discuss with an adult, and illustrate the differences between the two concepts. The illustrations are clipped together with large rings. Each week a different student shares their illustration and insight. Reporting on the assignment in this manner allows the concepts of discipline and self-discipline to be reviewed throughout the school year.

When such an assignment was given, one child drew two bumper cars. In the first car, an adult was behind the steering wheel driving a child. The student explained that, when you need to be disciplined, you are not responsible to do things alone. In the second drawing, a child was behind the wheel to indicate self-discipline had been acquired.

In another illustration, a student drew two stick figures. The first stick figure showed arrows coming from the outside pointing inward to indicate that directives on how to act came from authority. In the second illustration, the arrows were pointing out of the stick figure to represent that when you learn to be self-disciplined, you choose the best way to act. Once the concepts were introduced, students were instructed in the *wait, think, act* process used to develop self- discipline. The 15-skills framework was shared. Students were informed that throughout the year they would be given information about each skill and challenged to practice the skills.

Teach Four Skills at the Beginning of School

The skills of Listening, Following Instructions, Understanding Reasons for Rules and Resolving Problems will be integral in any productive group situation. These four skills are imbedded in the 15-skills framework and are both skills used when disciplining as well as skills taught as self-discipline. On the illustrated skill chart on p. 24 you will notice these four skills form an 'L.' The 'L' reminds us that there are limits to what is acceptable and unacceptable. A deliberate review of these four skills at the beginning of the school year can eliminate disruption and student's uncertainty of teacher expectations. Whatever is ignored or tolerated the first few weeks of school will linger throughout the school year.

These skills are normally addressed as part of your classroom management plan. Effective teachers address these four skills even if they do not know about DWP or the 15-skills framework. Only after instructional control has been established will these four skills be introduced as skills students learn to acquire to become self-disciplined. A *DWP* teacher will wait until students understand that these four essential elements are needed for the teacher to be able to teach and the students able to learn. The minimum information given about each of the four skills is listed below.

Skill # 1 – Listening:

- Teach the six steps of listening (Chapter 4).
- Develop a class listening cue (Chapter 4).
- Distinguish focused listening, a self-discipline skill from other types of listening (Chapter 4).

Skill #2 – Following Instructions:

- Give instructions using multiple modalities: say, write, draw.
- Coach students to ask three questions before following instructions (Chapter 5).
- o Do I know what to do?
- o Do I know how to do it?
- o How much time will I have to complete the task?

Skill #7 – Understanding the Rules:

- Provide students with a copy of the classroom rules (Chapter 11).
- Let students develop T-charts. On one side, list acceptable procedures (looks like/sounds like) to follow the rules; on the other side, list unacceptable procedures.

Skill #12 – Resolving Problems:

- Describe to students the three to five-step plan used when rules are not followed or when behaviors are dangerous, disruptive, or disrespectful (Chapter 17).
- Role-play the appropriate and inappropriate ways to accept correction.
- If documentation in the form of an action plan is one of the steps in the your classroom management, teach students how to fill out the plan. Specific statements such as "I'll bring all supplies to class" are more productive than, "I'll try harder."

CHAPTER 4

The Skill of Listening

The Chambered Nautilus was chosen for its ear-like shape and multi-chambered body to suggest the skill of listening. If we really listen to one another, we can experience a kind of resonance in mind and thought.

When we LISTEN

We WAIT to speak.

We THINK: Do I understand what the speaker is saying? Do I have a question? Can I do what is suggested?

We ACT: We ask a question, repeat what was said, and/or do the task.

The first five days of third grade went remarkably well for first-year teacher Marti. At the start of the second week, she noticed her students took longer to focus their attention. Side conversations broke out and students talked even when she tried to give instructions.

A fellow teacher offered Marti a list of the 15 self-discipline skills, along with a brief explanation of the Basic Skills. When Marti looked at the list, she realized she had not talked with her class about any of the first five skills, especially the first one. She had assumed her students would know how to listen and believed her main job was to show that she was a teacher who cared about them and the subjects being taught. When Marti asked her 28 third graders, "Do you know what I expect you to do when I ask you to listen?" a few students ventured answers. "We should open our ears and close our mouths;" "Make sure our ears are clean so we can hear you;" "We should follow your instructions."

Marti took 15 minutes to show and tell her expectations for how students listen. She told them there were three things they would have to do to get ready to listen:

1. Stop moving and talking.
2. Clear away distractions (this usually means to take everything out of your hands).
3. Look at or toward the person speaking.

She also told them that she knew they could do these three steps without listening. She introduced them to three actions that show they had listened.

1. Ask questions about what was said.
2. Say in their own words what they heard.
3. If a direction was given, as soon as the speaker was finished, begin the task.

She invited the students to ask *every* question they had about listening. They role-played the right way and the wrong way to listen. She put a masking tape X on the floor in the front and center of the classroom. Marti told her students that whenever someone was standing on the X, it was a cue to show their listening position by completing the first three steps of the skill. Each child made a postcard listing the six steps of listening to keep on his or her desk.

Marti taught, coached, cued, practiced, recognized, and complimented students as they demonstrated mastery of the first self-discipline skill. "What a difference it makes when you don't assume a group of children will know what you expect when you ask them to listen," she said. Not all of Marti's students had the ability to demonstrate all six steps of listening on their own. Some needed a partner or buddy to remind them when it was time to listen. But all of Marti's students knew when someone asked them to listen, it was time to be quiet and focus. Teachers are under constraints of time, testing, curriculum standards, and behavior management. Despite this, Marti realized she had to stop and take time to address the listening skill. In doing so, she recaptured time by not having to address the listening issue repeatedly.

Six Steps of Listening

The first and most essential skill that helps children *wait, think, and act* is the skill of listening. Parents begin training young children in the steps of listening when they take a child's chin and gently turn her face to look at them. Teachers train preschoolers to stop and listen when they teach them to "freeze," or turn lights on and off as a signal to stop moving and talking. We train children from kindergarten through third grade by teaching them the six steps in listening. Teachers know that listening without prompts or cues will be difficult for children five years of age through third grade.

HOW TO LISTEN

1. **STOP** what you are doing or saying.

2. **CLEAR AWAY** distractions.

3. **LOOK AT OR TOWARD** the person speaking.

4. **TELL** the person what you heard them say.

5. **ASK QUESTIONS** about what you heard.

6. **DO THE TASK** you hear a person ask you to do.

Six-year-old Sarah applied at home the listening skills she was learning at school. Her parents knew about the six steps of listening from the first home-and-school meeting. One afternoon, Sarah's mom told her she was going to the garage to finish a project and if she needed her, she could find her there. Not more than five minutes later, Sarah was crying and shouting, "Mom, Mom, where are you?" Her mom rushed in to calm her fears. "I couldn't find you," said Sarah, crying. "But honey, didn't you hear me tell you I would be in the garage?" Frustrated, Sarah asked, "Was I looking at you?" "No" said her mother. "Then I wasn't listening."

There are six steps people use when listening. A child learns the first three steps (stop, clear away, look) must be completed quickly when an adult gives them a signal or asks them to listen. In school, waiting until everyone is ready gives children the chance to practice impulse control. The wording of the first three steps changes when taught to older students:

- Calm yourself. Get into a comfortable position.
- Clear away mental and physical distractions.
- Direct your attention to the action. (speaker, film, computer, etc.)

Adults know that children can stop what they are doing or saying, clear their distractions and face forward; however, these actions alone will not guarantee listening. For this reason, there are three additional actions that indicate listening has occurred. A speaker knows if someone has listened if:

- what was said can be repeated or paraphrased;
- questions on the topic are asked;
- students follow directions given.

When we name and compliment students who demonstrate the last three steps of listening, we reinforce that, while one *waits and listens,* one also *thinks* about what is said.

Make Listening a Habit

To make the skill of listening habitual, adults use a listening cue to gain focused attention. Examples of cues include:

- When a speaker raises a hand, students will raise their hands, stop talking, and wait for everyone to refocus.
- When a speaker says, "If you can hear my voice, clap once. If you can hear my voice, clap twice." The group responds with two claps and then silently moves into a listening position.
- A teacher might say, "Please stack your blocks." This is the cue to face forward, put your back straight in the chair, and place your feet firmly on the ground indicating these three blocks of your body are in alignment.
- Older students can design the word or cue they want their teachers to use. One group of fourth graders came up with the word "salame," which stood for "stop and look at me."

A habit is a recurrent behavior done unconsciously. Research suggests it can take from 21 to 60 days to form a new habit (Popova, "How Long It Takes to Form a New Habit"). Adults who intentionally teach students to listen, coach children to use the six steps multiple times a day for a minimum of two weeks. Children remain in their listening positions while instructions are given, important messages are read, and information is disseminated. When the time to listen is over, normal activity resumes. When invited to listen using the six steps outlined here, the speaker should tell the group how long to remain in their listening positions. As a rule of thumb, teachers were coached to speak a maximum of one minute per age of the group. *DWP* teachers have observed today's children are often not able to remain in a listening position for more than half that time.

Making Eye Contact

In most Western cultures, eye contact is a basic ingredient of effective communication. Many classrooms consist of children from multiple cultures and some cultures consider it impolite to look an adult in the eye. We adjusted by rephrasing the third step of listening to "look at or toward the speaker." In this way, we felt confident of accommodating and not offending anyone.

Primary children are taught the rhyme, "If my eyes you cannot see, don't begin to talk to me." This rhyme is not so much about looking someone in the eye as it is a reminder *not* to shout to people who might be in another room.

Different Types of Listening

As students age developmentally, adults and teachers can introduce the sub-classes of listening which are:

Focused listening: When a self-discipline skill is practiced using the six steps of listening.

Appreciative listening: When we listen to music or a reading.

Discriminative listening: When we distinguish facts from feelings and opinions.

Comprehensive listening: When we try to understand what a speaker says.

Therapeutic listening: When we serve as a sounding board without passing judgment.

Critical listening: When we listen and plan to evaluate what we heard.

Students can evaluate their listening ability by asking four questions:

- What is the entire lesson about? (Comprehensive listening)
- What are the main ideas? (Discriminative listening)

- Are the speaker's conclusions sound or mistaken? (Critical listening)
- What does the lesson mean to me? (Appreciative listening)

Tips for Teaching Listening

As teachers and parents taught the six steps of listening, they shared their insights through the *DWP* newsletter and in follow-up sessions. We received feedback from teachers and students as follows:

(3rd Grade Teacher) "To prompt a child in kindergarten through third grade to be self-disciplined, I say, "Please *show me* your listening power or listening skill." Using the directive "show me" reminds the child there are action steps they must choose to use"

(Music Teacher) "To help young children remember the steps of listening, we learned the "Listening Song" created by teacher Jo Mersnick and sung to the tune of "Frére Jacques" sometimes called, "Brother John" or "Are You Sleeping?"

The Lyric to the Listening Song

Are you listening? Are you listening?
I hope so. I hope so.
Can you sing the six steps?
Can you sing the six steps?
Ready, set go! Ready, set go!
Stop what you're doing.
Stop what you're doing.
Clear things away. Clear things away.
Turn toward the speaker.
Turn toward the speaker.

Repeat what they say. Repeat what they say.
Think things over. Think things over.
Ask your questions. Do the task too.
These are all the six steps.
These are all the six steps.
That I can do. That I can do.

(2nd Grade Teacher) "I know now that I have to wait for silence before beginning a lesson or to speak to my class. My class and I take time to get into a listening position. Use professional judgment about how long you should wait. If students are just learning the skill, try to wait until everyone is ready. Compliment those who are in the neutral position ready to learn. Once you have identified the children who cannot get into a listening position quickly, assign them a partner. Let the partner coach or assist them in putting things away. Remind yourself that listening is a skill like any other skill."

(4th Grade Teacher) "I remind students when they choose to listen, there will be a benefit to them and everyone else in the group. This helps them to think altruistically and can serve as a motivator for those who have difficulty listening."

(5th Grade Teacher) "My indicators for successful teaching of the skill of listening include:

- If the class can respond quickly to the listening cue.
- If students demonstrate tolerance for the opinion of others and a willingness to listen.
- If students infrequently request that verbal directions are repeated.
- If students have a sufficient attention span for the task at hand."

After learning about the skill of listening, a busy parent confessed that the only time she asks her children to listen is when she has something negative to say to them. "First," she said, "I have to work on this skill when my children ask me to listen... Secondly, I'm going to make a point of saying something positive to my children when I ask them to use this type of focused listening. I know we can get better at this skill if we work together."

The Last Word

The US Department of Health and Human Services estimates that American children spend a whopping seven-hours a day in front of electronic media. According to the Michigan State University Extension, excessive TV viewing is linked to delays in cognitive, linguistic, and social-emotional skills in young children. Screen time can also be a predictor of poor executive functioning and self-control in children (Rymanowicz, "Screen Time for Young Children). A drought in the person-to-person contact in the American home can make listening a difficult skill. The most basic sign of respect one human being can give to another is to still their own activity and concentrate on the other person when listening. It is no accident that the words 'silent' and 'listen' contain the same letters.

Paula's Story

While I devoted my time to developing the *Discipline with Purpose* program, Paula left Boys Town to work in an inner-city school where she tested ways to teach self-discipline to high school students. When school ended in May, Paula gave her students a class celebration. Together they reviewed the year and reflected on the best and the 'not so good' lessons they had together. At the end of the hour, Paula spoke heart-to-heart to her students. She prompted them to continue reading over the summer and to keep up their friendships, ending with this, "Promise me one thing. Promise me you will keep your guns at home when you are out on the streets." It was the height of gang warfare in North Omaha.

Three weeks after school ended, a news report carried information about a local student shot by a gang member in the hospital with wounds but not in critical condition. When Paula found out it was one of her students, she immediately went to visit him. When she entered the room, Tim sat up. Before she could even say anything, he said, "Mrs. Lenz, I didn't listen to you!" She sat with Tim and got his side of the story giving comfort where able.

Reflecting on this exchange, Paula remarked that by using those five words "I didn't listen to you," Tim had acknowledged, perhaps for the first time, that there was a voice in his life worth listening to.

Post-Script

Unfortunately, the pressures of his environment did not allow him to sustain the ability to listen to someone who cared. When Tim was 18 and within a few months of leaving high school, he was incarcerated. Paula visited him in prison until he was moved to another facility where she was unable to keep track of him. Reflecting on Tim, Paula will tell you that even today, the memory of Tim evokes sadness and a sense of powerlessness.

CHAPTER 5

The Skill of Following Instructions

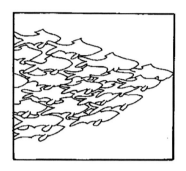

A group of fish that stays together for social reasons is said to be shoaling. When fish swim in the same direction together, it is schooling. Fish swim in schools for a variety of reasons including safety, to search for food, or to breed. Swimming in the same direction ensures the good for each and all.

When we FOLLOW INSTRUCTIONS:

We WAIT for the speaker to finish giving directions.

We THINK: Do I know what to do? What questions do I have? Do I have a plan? If not, what should I do? How much time will I have to finish?

We ACT: We move quickly to begin following instructions.

This story may be an old joke, but the point is clear. A young mother had three young boys all under the age of seven. So, listening and following instructions were two skills she wanted her children to practice. One day, while doing laundry, she noticed that there was only one pair of socks in the wash for each of her children for three days. She instructed each of her children to change their socks every day. Each child agreed. A week later on laundry day she noticed that, once again, there was only one pair of socks per child. She asked the children why they didn't change socks as she had asked them to do. "But we did," said the oldest. "Tommy gave me his and I gave him mine." When she asked the youngest, he too said he had changed his socks. "I put the sock I wore yesterday on my left foot and I put the other one on my right foot and changed them every day."

Following instructions is a two-way event. It is a dual responsibility of the giver of instructions to make the instructions clear and the receiver to clarify what has been said. Listeners should be offered the opportunity to ask questions about what they heard, repeat the instructions in their own words, and show the speaker how to follow the instructions.

What is Necessary for Persons to Follow Instructions?

Learning to follow instructions requires attentiveness, the ability to understand concepts and vocabulary, and the ability to work on a task without distractions, sustaining this effort until task completion. It is difficult for a young child to *wait*. Since children have a variety of learning styles, this skill can be taught in a number of ways. Here are strategies adults can use to teach children how to follow instructions:

- Ask the student to demonstrate the first three steps of listening before giving instructions. Teachers coach children to calm their bodies and minds by playing soft music or they use a chime to indicate it is time to become calm.
- Assign a coach to students who need additional help. The coach can be a peer, an older student, or an adult.
- Avoid issuing an instruction without looking to see if the person is ready to hear the message.
- Explain tasks clearly and simply.
- List the steps on a sheet of paper or on the board or have students list them. Say aloud one, two, three as a key word or the step is listed. Try to limit instructions to three steps; when these are accomplished, list three more.
- Demonstrate how the task might be accomplished. Encourage the coach to show the students how to complete assignments by modeling a step-by-step approach while verbally explaining each step.
- Ask children to practice or tell you how they plan to proceed.
- Inquire about additional unanswered questions children might have.
- Ask students to set a personal goal indicating the tasks they can complete in one minute. Often students perform beyond their prediction.
- Set a time for completing the steps assigned. Negotiate by asking how much time a group thinks they will need to finish an assignment.

- Go over the completed task and evaluate the progress made.
- Engage students in experiential activities that demonstrate how enjoyable it can be to follow instructions (See suggested activities on pages 47-49).

Difficulties in Following Directions

Young children will sometimes refuse to listen to instructions or will engage only in activities of their choosing. They may look blankly at you and appear to be non-compliant or try to distract you by bringing up other topics. These behaviors can indicate physical difficulties. A child may need hearing or speech therapy. Inattention can be due to psychological issues more difficult to detect. What is on the child's mind? Did something happen before they came to school? Did they have a healthy breakfast? Is there a language barrier? In these cases, the adult is the one who must *stop* and *think* before *acting.*

A child will have difficulty following instructions if the task seems overwhelming. This can happen when too many verbal instructions are given at once. It can also happen when a child needs constant reassurance from an adult to complete the task. Adults can present instructions in short simple directives and repeat the directives as often as needed. Check that the information requested is accurately understood.

One strategy to help children in these situations is to set an independent goal, stating how much they think they can accomplish in the time allotted. If the child has no concept of time, use an egg timer or stopwatch to help the student learn what they can accomplish in one minute. Children are usually amazed at the progress they can make if they stay focused for the entire minute.

Older students accomplish tasks better when they participate in the planning. Pretest students so those who have mastered the material can complete independent work. Ask yourself these questions: 1) Is the student motivated to work on this task? 2) How does it impact or relate to the student's life? 3) How will following instructions and completing the task help the student?

If there are no medical issues, there are three reasons learners do not follow instructions: 1) The child does not know what to do; 2) The child does not know how to perform the task; 3) The child is not motivated. The following phrases or ones similar in content will help reinforce the skill:

- Does everyone know *what* to do? If you are not sure, this is the perfect time to ask a question.
- Does everyone know *how* to do the assignment? Who can tell the first thing you plan to do when I stop talking? Does someone have a different plan they can share?
- How much time will you have to complete this task? Set a goal for yourself even if you don't think you can complete the entire task... I can give you up to 20 minutes for this task. How much time would you like?

A lack of motivation can be a long-term issue. Children may see no relationship between the task and themselves. They may have low self-confidence and low expectations for success, as well as fear of success or failure and achievement anxieties. Many motivational issues have been resolved by using the Two-By-Ten Technique, a strategy to improve the teacher-student relationship.

Spend two minutes a day for ten days straight talking with your most challenging student about anything he or she wants to discuss. Look back at the student's interest inventory form and identify hobbies, interests, likes, dislikes, etc. to give you a starting point, or design one to be used. Allow the student to take the lead. Ask questions and listen carefully to the response.

At first, it may feel awkward trying to think of things to talk about when discussions about academics, grades, and discipline are off-limits.

A word of caution: students know when you are being real. If your goal is to get to know the student, your authenticity will come through and the student will trust the connection you are trying to make. If your goal is to get them to do something for you (behave better), your attempt at manipulation will only further push students away. Improved attitude and behavior are by-products of a stronger teacher-student relationship.

Teachers must be intentional about creating opportunities to implement this strategy, because it will not happen simply by waiting for an opportunity to present itself. You may want to partner with another teacher to accomplish this task (Kassi, 2017).

Teach the Skill Using Experiential Activities

Following instructions is introduced to primary students as the second "Hidden Power." When teachers introduce the skill, they engage students in fun experiential activities. One example is Simon Says, an easy game to play. Children line up in front of the leader who will be Simon. They are told that Simon will give them directions to follow. If they hear "Simon says" before a statement, the players should follow the instructions. If they do *not* hear "Simon says" before the instruction, they should disregard the instruction.

The game starts with a simple one-step direction such as, "Simon says clap your hands." In the beginning, Simon can demonstrate the directions with the players. Later, Simon can stop demonstrating and verbalize multi-step instructions. For example, "Simon says clap your hands, then hop on one foot, and (finally) sit on the floor." Typically, students are out of the game when they make a mistake. The teacher directs them to return to their places and write or draw the directions they were unable to follow in their Hidden Skills booklets. Teachers repeat this game whenever students need a short stretch break or another opportunity to practice the skill.

Young children have difficulty following more than three verbal instructions. They tend to do the last two actions and forget about the first. When Tonya, a second-grade teacher, introduced the skill to her students, she asked for volunteers who wanted to *practice* following instructions. The selected volunteers were asked how many oral instructions they would like to follow. They would have to remember the instructions but need not complete them in order. In one case, a volunteer asked for three instructions. Tonya's instruction was, "When I stop talking, go over and knock on the door once, print your name on the board, and hop back to your seat. Please begin." The room was silent as all the students watched the volunteer. The actions were completed in order and efficiently. When the volunteer paused to think for a moment, several students wanted to offer help. As soon as the activity was finished, hands shot up in the air. "I want to try. I want to try," students shouted. Tonya said, "We only have time for two more people to practice the skill today, but we will continue to practice." That day, students gathered around the teacher during recess. To Tonya's surprise, the students chanted, "Can we practice following instructions? Can we practice following instructions?" The teacher said, "Of course," and created simple, safe actions for the students to follow.

Another simple exercise is Stand Up, Sit Down, a useful game for all ages. The teacher reads aloud the story "The Colorful Shoes," (found below) but first gives these instructions:

Every time you hear a word that begins with the letter 'C' stand up. Stay standing until you hear a word that begins with an 'F' and then sit down. Stay seated until you hear another word that begins with a 'C' and stand up again. Repeat this process until the story is finished. Invite questions to clarify the instructions. Participants often ask if we are listening for the sound of 'C' or 'F' or the actual letter. Compliment the person for asking a question others might want answered, and tell them they are to listen for words that begin with the letter 'C' and 'F.'

The Colorful Shoes

One day I was in the school *cafeteria* eating my lunch with all the other students. I was using my *fork* and my knife to *cut* some beets which were *floating* in red juice, when to my surprise, the beets took off and landed right on my teacher's shoes. My teacher had just bought the shoes and they had *cost* her a lot of money. They had high heels and were very *fancy*. They had started out as a pretty *color* of blue, but now they were beet-red. They really looked sort of *funny*, but I didn't laugh because I noticed a *crabby* expression on my teacher's *face*. "I'm sorry," I said. "The beets slid off my plate and I just *couldn't* help it." Her *frown* went away. She smiled and looked down at her shoes. "They really are *colorful* now," she said. "Blue and red are my *favorite colors*." I'm not sure she meant it, but it made me *feel* a lot better (Used with Permission from *Play by The Rules* (1990) by Greta Rasmussen).

Assign older students the task of creating additional paragraphs to be read to the class. Students can create paragraphs in which others listen for nouns and verbs, items made of wood or metal, green vegetables or red fruits, or even capitals of states versus cities that are not. Students decide when the listeners must stand or sit. This exercise provides a way of following instructions infused with language arts, geography, or other subjects. In this assignment, students practice the skills of listening, following instructions, and independently accomplishing tasks.

Pre-teach Expectations

Pre-teaching is the planned and conscious discussion of expected behaviors before an event takes place. The adult anticipates the *who, what, when, where,* and *why* questions and talks about each so children can feel secure in new situations. As a preventative measure, pre-teaching can help adults anticipate potential challenges.

One mother shared her pre-teaching story on preparing her family to dine out. "Tonight, we are going out to eat as a family. We have all had a busy week and this will be a great way to spend some time together. Mom and Dad have chosen the restaurant this time. You will have a chance to select one the next time. There will be lots of instructions to follow tonight, so let me tell you about some of them.

"When we get to the restaurant, we may have to wait for a table. Sometimes there are places to sit and wait, but sometimes we have to stand. While we are waiting for the table, we can talk, but we cannot run around or be loud. Once we are sitting at the table, it is important that we show our table manners and talk in voices that do not disrupt others. If I see that you are having trouble waiting or you are disrupting others, I will give you a reminder by counting from one to three. Once I reach the number three, we will have to leave. That means you and I will sit in the car and wait for the rest of the family to finish dinner. Who can tell me one instruction you must follow? What would be a reason I will start counting to three? What will happen if I reach the number three? Now, ask me questions about what we are going to do."

This mother capitalized on the simple explanation of pre-teaching offered to parents in the school take-home newsletter. A suggestion was made that parents look for one opportunity to use this method to help children achieve success in following instructions. The mom reported that after reaching the number two with one of her children and the number one with another, everyone enjoyed the meal and the children were eager to offer restaurants for the next night out.

Use Poetry to Highlight the Skill

Invite students to create other poems about instructions that can teach lessons about life.

Beware of Coat Zippers
by Christine Ryktarsyk

I have some information.
That I think you all should know.
It has to do with zippers
On coats you wear for snow.
When the weather gets quite nippy
And the winds begin to blow,
Don't zip your coat up quickly
Or your tears will start to flow.
You will zip your lip, I tell you,
Or you'll zip your neck, oh no!
Don't zip your coat up quickly
When you zip your coat, zip slow.

The Last Word

Of the five basic self-discipline skills, primary children have said they see adults listening, sharing, questioning, and using our social skills, but they do not see us practice the skill of following instructions. Children believe adults *give* instructions but do not need to follow them. It is important to relate the reasons why this Basic Skill serves people for a lifetime.

Simple Routines Build Respect

A group of teachers visited an elementary school where children had been learning about the 15 self-discipline skills for several years. Each visitor spent about ten to fifteen minutes in a primary, intermediate, or junior high classroom. They had many good things to say during the lunch debriefing. One thing they noticed was how kind the teachers were toward the students. "What did you see or hear?" asked the facilitator of the group. The observers noted the teachers kept asking the students, "How much time do you think you will need to finish this assignment?" or "I can give you ten minutes to work on this project. Some of you may not finish, but do the best you can."

FOLLOWING INSTRUCTIONS

Before doing this skill ask yourself:

1. **Do I know WHAT to do?**
2. **Do I know HOW to do it?**
3. **How much TIME do I have to finish the task?**

The observers referred to the three questions routinely asked when giving assignments: Do you know *what* to do? Do you know *how* to do it? How much *time* will you need to finish?

The teachers had a long discussion about the benefits of delaying a child's impulsive need to begin work as soon as a task was assigned. They liked the idea of waiting until three questions were answered. In a primary classroom, teachers observed students taking the responsibility to ask themselves these questions during independent work time. Each student had a small card and was asked to stand and listen while instructions were given. After hearing the verbal instructions, they referred to the card. When they could answer all the questions, they began work. The classroom teacher knew immediately who needed remedial help and moved from one student to the next until all were seated. The card was used to help students stop and think before beginning work. The illustration on the card reminded children they could move straight ahead once the questions were answered.

As teachers built a routine to help students *wait* and *think* before rushing through an assignment, they demonstrated their desire for all the youngsters to succeed in following instructions. What the observers saw was a mutually respectful attitude between students and teacher.

"In any given circumstance of life, we have the alternative of stopping and thinking before acting – the alternative of restraint. Instead of unthinkingly rushing into action, we can ask ourselves:

Do I really want to do this?
Is anybody going to be hurt by this?
Will I like having done this?"

Choosing Civility, P.M. Forni, p. 22

Hand Gestures Used to Help Remember the Skills of Self-Discipline

1. *Listening* – Cup hands over ears.
2. *Following Instructions* – Make your fingers do the walking.
3. *Asking Questions* – Make a question mark in the air.
4. *Sharing* – Pretend you are passing out papers.
5. *Exhibiting Social Skills* – Shake your own hand up and down.
6. *Cooperating* – Interlock your thumbs and index fingers.
7. *Understanding Reasons for Rules* – Pretend you are directing traffic.
8. *Accomplishing a Task* – Pretend you are combing your hair.
9. *Exhibiting Leadership* – Raise your hand indicating you will take the lead.
10. *Communicating Effectively* – Use your thumbs and index fingers to pretend you are texting.
11. *Organizing* – Tap your left wrist four times while saying "Time, Space, People, and Things."
12. *Resolving Problems* – Show the peace sign using two fingers.
13. *Initiating Solutions* – Cross your arms to think; then, hold up one finger like a light bulb went off in your head.
14. *Distinguishing Fact from Feeling* – Draw a heart on your chest to indicate empathy.
15. *Sacrificing/Serving Others* – Show both palms as if offering to help another.

CHAPTER 6

The Skill of Asking Questions

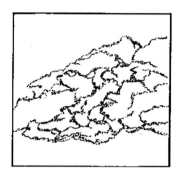

Looking at clouds often makes us question what we see without eyes as well as without imagination. Questioning can give us thought for possibilities we might not have previously imagined. The skies signal movement, urging us to view the world through a new paradigm.

When we ASK QUESTIONS:

We WAIT for a speaker to finish speaking.

We THINK: Am I curious about anything the speaker has said? What words will I use to ask my question?

We ACT: We ask to be recognized by the speaker.

When Isidor Isaac Rabi, the 1944 Nobel Prize winner in Physics, was asked about the major influences in his life, he told the story about growing up in Brooklyn.

When his friends came home from school, their parents asked them, "What did you learn in school today?" When Isidor came home from school each day, his mother asked him, "Izzy, did you ask a good question today?" Isidor told how that daily question from his mother helped him develop the inquisitive mind necessary for academic success and his eventual scientific discoveries (Sheff, 1988, *New York Times*).

Of the first five skills, asking questions appropriately can be the hardest for children to accomplish if they are not fully engaged in the activity. Young children tend to tell their stories and make statements about topics. It is difficult for them to stay focused on the big picture. They often get sidetracked with elements of a story that pique their curiosity. Frequently, they do not know the words *who, what, when, why, where,* and *how* are good to use when asking questions. Almost all children need to learn the criteria for asking questions and the times when questions might embarrass, be awkward or inappropriate.

"Are you pregnant?"

"Are you wearing a wig?"

"How much money do you make?"

When children have not learned or are not motivated to practice the skill of asking questions, they exhibit the following behaviors:

- The same questions are asked repeatedly.
- Shy students fail to get their questions answered because they are afraid to speak in front of a group.
- Questions are asked at inappropriate times or are embarrassing to a speaker.
- Students rely on teachers to answer questions rather than seek out answers.
- Students cannot ask for what they need.

Other factors contribute to children having difficulty with the third self-discipline skill. Sometimes, focused listening is poorly established, preventing a person from hearing a message. In school, experience may have taught students that teachers will answer questions when asked out-of-turn or blurted out. This will discourage serious students, and those who process more slowly, from participating. It is the teacher's responsibility to provide students with a clear procedure for asking questions that will also help draw out the shy or reticent student. Teachers ask questions they assume are clear, but students may have different viewpoints. As teachers, we can ask ourselves if it is acceptable to allow students to question us. How do we receive their questions? Do we encourage curiosity as well as challenging and thought-provoking questions?

Strategies that Encourage Questions

Provide 'wait' and 'think' time after asking a question. Silently count to 20 and direct students to keep thinking about how they want to respond, until they hear you say aloud, "Seventeen, 18, 19, 20, all hands up please." Pause before asking a group question. Look around the room. Pretend you are thinking. Say aloud, "Let's see... whose I.Q. points should we tap today?" Then, call upon someone to respond. Walk around the room. Tell children the one you tap on the shoulder will be the person who can give the first answer.

Using a small paper box, develop question cubes that have one of these words *who, what, where, why, how,* and *when* printed on each side. Students toss the cube and practice formulating questions using the word that lands on the top. For older students, print the words on stand-up cards. Place one or two question cards on the desks of three or four students. Challenge teams to generate five to ten questions on a topic that begin with the word printed on the question card.

Show excitement when thought-provoking questions are asked or answered. Clap. Do a cheer. Run to the board and write the question or answer. Offer to give the student an imaginary million-dollar check or hand them a 20-dollar bill in play money. Encourage intellectual curiosity whenever possible.

Print the names of your students on sticks. Tell the class that everyone will have a chance to participate throughout the day. Each time the teacher asks a question, one or more sticks will be pulled out of the cup. At the end of the day, each person who did not answer a question is asked one that pertains to the day's activities.

Some students think of a question right in the middle of a presentation. To help students *wait,* place a sticky note on each desk. Direct all students to record questions as they think of them. Questions can be open, closed, yes, no - anything goes. At the end of a lesson invite students to ask their questions. If time does not permit you to answer all of them, direct students to post their note in the 'parking lot.' A 'parking lot' is a section of a board where these post-it notes can remain until questions are answered. Reserve a few minutes each day to attend to the questions posted in the parking lot.

Asking Too Many Questions

When learners lack confidence in their ability to complete work, they may ask too many questions and need help discerning questions they can answer on their own. Place question marks on ice-cream sticks or cardboard strips. Give the child having difficulty six to eight question sticks. Tell the child you will ask for one of the sticks each time they need a question answered. Direct them to *wait* and *think* because many of the questions they will be able to answer for themselves. If they lose all their sticks, they will have to answer their own questions until it is time to distribute the sticks again. Determine the length of time developmentally appropriate for the age and need of the child. Children can determine the number of questions sticks they need as they gain more self-confidence in their ability to answer their own questions.

ASKING QUESTIONS

Helpful questions are those that.........

- the speaker hasn't already answered.
- **have not been asked before.**
- other people want answered too.
- are **phrased** well.
- make people **think.**
- make the speaker feel **comfortable** and not ill at ease.
- keep the conversation **on the topic.**
- are not **stallers.**
- are not **statements in disguise.**

Different Types of Questions

Teach students five different types of questions. Then, place an object in a box and ask students to use the information to formulate questions that will help them identify the item.

1. Shape questions: Is it round? Is it flat? Is it square?
2. Weight questions: Is it heavy? Does it weigh more than an apple? Is it feather weight?
3. Size questions: Does it fit in a shoebox? Would it fit in my hand? Is it bigger than a baseball?

4. Action questions: Does it move? Can it move by itself? Is it alive? Will it roll?
5. Color questions: Is it red, black, etc.? Is it many different colors? Is it all one color?

Teach the Criteria for Effective Questioning

Respecting the privacy of others, an important social skill, is now fading from civil discourse. In this age of transparency, embarrassing questions typically asked privately are now aired in public. Children need to know how to ask appropriate questions and can be taught the criteria for effective questioning. Talk about the difference between a statement and question and discuss questions that a speaker might find uncomfortable. Teach students the phrase "Would it be uncomfortable or embarrassing if I asked you..." to use when unsure if their question is appropriate. The poster "Asking Questions" on Page 60 identifies the characteristics of an effective question.

Unnecessary Questions

Frustrated that his group of sixth graders were too impulsive about work, Mr. Overcamp came up with an idea. He privately invited three of his more reliable students to list questions they hear their classmates ask repeatedly. The list included the following:

What does this question mean?	Can I use the restroom?
What are we going to do today?	How many pages does it have to
When is this due?	be?
Should we print, write, or use a	Is this good enough?
computer?	When does this class end?

When the list was complete, the class starred every question they could answer for themselves. The list was posted and students were challenged to monitor the questions they asked by *waiting and thinking* before *asking* a question they could answer themselves.

Curiosity and Divergent Thinking

In 1956, Benjamin Bloom published a hierarchical ordering of cognitive skills designed to help teachers teach and students learn. Today this framework is used to frame digital tasks, evaluate apps, write questions and assessments, and most importantly, to design learning objectives for students. Teachers help students develop curiosity by asking questions that demonstrate divergent thinking or higher levels according to **Bloom's Taxonomy:**

Knowledge or Recall	A person is asked to define, describe, identify, list, match, or name information previously learned.
Comprehension or Interpretation	A person is asked to explain, summarize, predict outcomes, and effects after grasping the meaning of material.
Apply	A person is asked to apply rules, laws, methods, and theories by demonstrating, solving, changing, operating, and applying learned material to a new situation.
Analyze	A person is asked to clarify a larger body of information into relational parts.
Synthesize	A person is asked to put together, create, design, and rearrange a set of abstract concepts to form a new whole.
Evaluate	A person is asked to judge value based on criteria and supportive evidence.

Tips for Asking and Answering Questions

Anticipate a student's discontentment with an answer by saying, "I'm going to say something now, and you may not like my answer. I hope you will accept it and stop asking."

Avoid asking a question if you know the answer. Often, adults see and know what has happened and yet ask, "What did you do?" A better question is, "How will you fix this?"

Avoid questions that begin with "Why?" Children who have not yet developed a reflective way of thinking may not know why. Others are given an opportunity to make up reasons to avoid the consequences. It is better to state what you saw or heard and ask how something happened.

Avoid questions that seem to put another person down (e.g. "Can't you do anything right?").

Avoid questions that can be answered with one word or "yes" or "no" and those starting with, "Would you like to...?" Middle grade and junior high students are too tempted to respond with a negative answer.

Encourage questions by your posture and tone. Say, "Ask me *every* question you have about this topic," rather than, "Are there any questions?"

If you do not want to answer questions or are unsure of the motive behind a student's question, ask, "What will you do with this information?" or say, "That's personal. If you want to know, we can talk about it privately."

If you don't want to debate or argue an issue, ask, "What do you want me to say?" or "What do you think?" or "What do you think I will say?"

Give the student who wants to argue the last word by saying: "Mark, why don't you have the last word on this issue."

Motivating Second Graders to Ask Questions

When Ms. Przybocki first started teaching the self-discipline skills, she used one lesson every three weeks. Her second graders learned the six steps of listening and how to follow instructions. They made Hidden Skill booklets and recorded what they wanted to remember about each skill. After a skill was introduced, students had three weeks to practice all or parts of the skill. Each student determined individual goals that met their learning needs. In addition, Ms. Przybocki made a flip chart for her class. Each time she taught a lesson, she illustrated or wrote key words or ideas that she intended to review many times during the school year. On one page of her flip chart, with the children's help, she listed the criteria for asking good questions:

- Has not been asked before
- Begins with a 'w' or 'h.'
- Won't be embarrassing. I will ask, "Will it embarrass you if I ask..."
- Is on the topic.
- A person asks after they raise their hand.

Ms. Przybocki used this flip chart with the instruction on how to ask a question whenever someone in the room celebrated a birthday. The birthday child sat in a special birthday chair and then answered ten questions asked by different classmates. The questions could only be answered if they fit the criteria for a good question. When all questions were answered, the teacher invited the birthday person to name one safe action they would like the class to perform ten times. One child wanted the students to rub their bellies with one hand and the top of their heads with the other. Another child wanted the class to shake hands with ten different classmates. Finally, the class sang the birthday song to the student:

Be A Birthday Celebrity
(Tune: Modified version of 'This Old Man')

Be a birthday celebrity
Sit in the chair for all to see
And we'll ask you questions
Ten will do
In your birthday interview.

With a class of 28 children, Ms. Przybocki intentionally practiced the skill of asking appropriate questions at least 20 or more times during the year. Because the activity was a pleasant one, the children associated practicing the skill with a positive experience.

CHAPTER 7

The Skill of Sharing: Time, Space, People, Things

 These grassy reeds illustrate the skill of sharing time, space, people, and things. The nature of the reeds allows them to sway with the wind, symbolizing flexibility. They adjust to their environment but remain rooted; they bend rather than break.

Sharing is working side by side with one or more persons and on a common task. Sharing can mean that everyone gets equal parts, but it can also mean everyone should have what is sufficient for their needs. Children in kindergarten through third grade will have difficulty demonstrating this skill without prompts. The goals for the skill of sharing are as follows:

- Provide students with different ways to share time, space, people, and things.
- Maintain a clean and orderly environment.
- Help students share limited resources and raise awareness of times and places where resources are scarce.
- Encourage a respect for the privacy and belongings of others.
- Build interpersonal connectedness between and among people.

Ego-centered children can find sharing uncomfortable. They want to be first and believe the teacher should like them the best. If they raise their hands two or three times in a row, but the teacher calls upon someone else, they can feel deflated. The meaning and complexity of this skill will expand as a person matures. Genuine sharing creates connections.

One afternoon, two teachers pulled up to a school loading dock to unload boxes and materials for an upcoming workshop. They noticed two high school boys using a wall of the school building to practice tennis swings. As soon as the boys spotted the car, they left the area and walked about 25 feet away. They looked a little guilty. The teachers thought they weren't supposed to be in this area of the school grounds.

One presenter got out of the car and went over to the boys, reached out her hand, and introduced herself. The boys shook hands and told their names. The teacher said, "We noticed when we drove up that you were bouncing your tennis ball off the wall of the school. We are sorry that we had to interrupt your practice, but we need to use this space. It will only take us a short time to unload and then we will move our car." The boys immediately offered to help. "That would be super," said the teacher. With the boys' help, the 15-minute job was reduced to five. Once finished, the teachers complimented the boys on their willingness to share space and be of service to someone in need. "No problem," said one boy. "Glad to help," said the second. These two young men did not know about the 15 self-discipline skills; they had likely responded to adult modeling. In thanking the students, the presenter told the boys how sharing space and their time had been beneficial.

Sharing Time

When we SHARE TIME:

We WAIT our turn.

We THINK: How am I going to use the time when it is my turn?

We ACT: We see how high we can count or distract ourselves so we can wait patiently.

We give and take.

When the concept of 'FaceTime' first developed, people all over the world had a chance to connect or reconnect on a deeper level. Today, many children share their lives more through video-conferencing than in person. Sharing time with others allows us to share our lives.

Parents can make time each day, even five to ten minutes, to stop and be fully present to children. Reading stories, listening to problems, sharing events happening in the family, community, and the world are all activities that require shared time. In school, Show and Tell allows children a time to be center stage. One important time is morning sharing, which allows students to get to know their classmates and build trust and community in a safe setting. In morning sharing time, students tell classmates what is happening in their lives, their struggles, and joys. The teacher initiates morning sharing with a simple question, such as, "What did you do this weekend?" Students learn to listen without commenting, except when prompted to ask additional questions.

Sharing Space

When we SHARE SPACE:

We WAIT until others have moved out of the space we want to occupy.

We THINK: Am I too close to people so their space is not being honored?

We ACT: We adjust our position so we can honor everyone's space.

Children can have difficulty discerning where they end and another person begins. They may stand too close to another or need to back off when someone else is too close. *DWP* educators teach children that everyone has eighteen or more inches of imaginary space around them. This personal space or bubble moves when we move and helps to define an appropriate distance between people. When we get too close to others without their permission, we invade their space. Hugging, holding hands, or linking arms may be a space invasion unless both parties are agreeable to these activities. Everyone has a right to have his or her personal space honored by others.

A most basic principle of sharing space is our voice and how it can affect others. Many loud and disruptive noises cannot be avoided. "Careful management of noise is a must for those who want to be civil" (Forni 2002, p. 93). Even before a child reaches kindergarten age, parents teach young children the difference between an *inside* voice and *an outside* voice. Talking on cell phones when in public can disrupt civil discourse and erode respect for others. Three strategies to teach shared space are as follows:

- Divide areas in the classroom, school, or home into sections. Assign individuals or groups of children to keep a section clean. Periodically assign an inspector to monitor the areas and give a progress report on neatness.

- Make the concept of sharing space more concrete for young children. Give each child a large sheet of newsprint (2x3 feet) and invite them to create a personal design on the paper that revolves around the theme of space. Laminate the mats when they are finished. Teach the children to bring the space mat when sitting in groups on the floor. The amount of space they should occupy is defined by their personal space mat. A smaller version of the mat can be made for use at the lunch table or media center. Older youngsters might be invited to share their time to help make space mats with the younger students.
- Autistic children and children who have social processing difficulties often stand too close. Give the child a hula hoop or smaller ring-shaped item and ask them to stand in the hoop about four feet away. Invite them to advance toward you one or two steps at a time. Stop and ask them to describe how they feel. Share your feelings regarding the closeness of space. Continue this process until you reach a comfortable distance. Use the term "arm's distance" to describe the appropriate personal space.

Teachers can place painting tape on the floor to surround their desk. Students are told to stand on the tape and *wait* for the teacher to invite them up to the desk. This helps students understand the teacher's desk is private space and students should not surround it when they want the teacher's attention.

> "One of the most elementary ways of being considerate is by respecting personal space. Leave enough room between yourself and others so that they won't feel uncomfortable or intimidated... Standing at an appropriate distance from others is part of poise, which gives strength and authority to your words."
>
> Choosing Civility, P.M. Forni, p. 100

Sharing People

*When we **SHARE PEOPLE**,*

*We **WAIT** until the person is available to get his/her attention.*

*We **THINK:** Is there anything I can do to help myself?*

*We **ACT:** We ask another person or look up the information for ourselves.*

Primary children were asked to name individuals they liked spending alone time with. Parents, siblings, mentors, and friends were identified. They were then asked how they felt when the person they wanted attention from was busy or unable to share with them. One young lady quoted lyrics from a Rolie Polie Olie song: "Not right now, or maybe later, Seems to me, like maybe never." She not only captured the wait aspect of this situation but clearly reflected on her inner feelings.

Sharing the Teacher

Talk with learners about the need to share the teacher. Discuss how children feel when they must wait and share the teacher's time or need attention. These guidelines have been helpful for teachers and parents alike:

- When you are in a group and want an adult's attention, raise your hand and *wait* for your name to be called or acknowledged.
- Use the words, "Excuse me," if you need an adult's attention when they are speaking with someone else. An adult can raise an index finger indicating they have heard you and will be attentive soon.
- Designate a bell or noisemaker that can be used to alert others there is an emergency.
- If your teacher is busy and cannot give you attention, you can go to someone in the room who is wearing an "I Can Help" button and request help from them.
- The slogan *Three Before Me* is helpful in giving students guidelines for requesting a teacher's attention.

Ask yourself for help; try to figure things out. (1)
Ask a person next to you. (2)
Ask the classroom helper or aide. (3)
If you cannot get help, ask the teacher. (ME)

Sharing Friends

Some children establish friends easily while others tend to be loners and need encouragement to develop friendships. Friendships are fluid with children. Adults help young children understand not everyone will be a friend, but everyone deserves respect. As their circles of friendships grow, older children will deal with more complex issues.

For example, when one child promises a friend they will meet and a more desirable offer comes along, what responsibility does the child have to keep his promise? How do best friends invite others into their group? How can we share time with people who seem to have few friends? A group of fifth and sixth graders generated a list of actions that makes friendship easy and those that make it more difficult.

Makes it Easy to be a Friend	Makes it Difficult to be a Friend
Person knows my name.	Person calls me nicknames I don't like.
We like to do similar activities.	We have little in common.
Person says nice things to me.	Person gossips about me.
I live near the person.	Person lives far away from me.
We laugh a lot about funny things.	Person teases or bullies me.
Person is sensitive to my needs.	When others pick on people who are different.
Person helps me be better.	When the other person gets me in trouble.
You can count on the person to be there.	If a person skips out if a better offer comes along.
Person listens to me if I tell them to stop doing something	If the person ignores what I say and continues to do things I don't like.
Will admit when they are wrong.	If they won't take responsibility for their actions.
Acts appropriately for the situation.	Acts like a "baby" or inappropriately.
Person is honest and truthful.	If the person tells lies about me.

Sharing Things

When we SHARE THINGS,

We WAIT for others to finish using materials.

We THINK: What condition will the object be in when I get it? How can I make sure I return it in the same or better condition?

We ACT: We are careful with shared materials.

Learning to share has benefits into adulthood. For example, some adult communities gather to inventory tools. In a shared data base, they list hammers, reference books, shovels, electrical saws, etcetera, which they are willing to share with others. Simple rules are established: if you damage an item, you pay for it; and the amount of time to borrow an item is limited.

The participants no longer have a need to own every tool and share their tools with others. In the same way, online file-sharing programs have allowed researchers, scientists, and doctors to share information and vastly expand the knowledge base. Our technological world has brought people closer together; with this interconnectedness, sharing becomes a necessity.

Waiting while another takes a turn or finishes playing with an object can be a challenge for young children who have not been taught how to share their possessions. Some children have never had to share because parents provide items as desired.

A time when children may not want to share is when they receive gifts or something new. Protect their right to explore new items. Tie a ribbon or pin a tag on the object to let others know that this item is not yet ready to be shared. The person who owns the item should designate when it is time to let others use the object. Many a teenager has also benefited from using this process with their siblings.

Learning About Sharing Beyond Third Grade

Primary grade children learn to share time, space, people, and things. Intermediate and upper grade students learn to share responsibilities, information, cultures, and friends. Learning to share other cultures provides an opportunity for middle grade students to explore customs, traditions,

71

foods, practices, and stories of that culture. After the following Vietnamese legend was shared, students were asked to research and share information about another culture.

A Vietnamese Tet Legend

The Emperor Hung-Vuong told his 22 sons that the one who brought the most meaningful present to honor the gods of heaven and earth on New Year's Day (TET) would inherit the throne. Twenty-one of the sons went far to find precious gifts, but the youngest, Lieu, saw the ripe rice waving in the fields and felt it was so beautiful that nothing could be a better offering. So, he asked his wife to make two special rice cakes – one round to symbolize the sky and one square to symbolize the earth.

When the princes came with their gifts of elephant tusks, rhinoceros' horns, and other precious things, the emperor was pleased. When at last he tasted the two simple rice cakes offered by Lieu and was told their meaning, the emperor was overwhelmed by their delicacy and simplicity.

Emperor Hung-Vuong named the round cake Banh Day and the square one Banh Chung. Since that day, the rice cakes have been traditional gifts given during Tet.

Skill Vocabulary to Reinforce the Skill of Sharing

There are many opportunities throughout the day when teachers can infuse skill language. These phrases can help coach children to share space, time, people, and things

- "Please stay in your personal space."

- "This is your time. This is my time."

- "Monitor your voice in the space we share."

- "Please use inside/outside voices."

- "There is one teacher and 20 students. What are some ways we can share the teacher?"

- "We will need to share the hallway with other students. I need three volunteers to show me what that will look like and sound like.

- "We are short on music books today. Who would be willing to share?" - Used in grades K-4.

- "We are short on music books today. Who can initiate a solution to this problem?" – Used in grades 5-8.

A Gift from The Heart

The greatest sharing occurs when people offer simple gifts that come from the heart. Adults can miss the meaning of gifts given by children unless they look sensitively into the heart of the child. I recall the story of "Three Letters from Teddy," now published in a book by that name by Elizabeth Ballard.

Teddy was a fifth grader, not particularly bright, and often came to school with hair unwashed and spotted clothing. The teacher tried hard to relate to Teddy, but she just couldn't warm up to him. Students seemed to exclude him from teams and group work. Teddy's mother passed away at the end of his third grade. Despite poor grades, he was passed along four years in a row.

When the Christmas holiday came around, children brought gifts for the teacher and stood around her desk as she opened them. In the middle of the pile was a gift wrapped in a brown paper bag and stuck together with tape. A Christmas tree with red bells had been drawn on the paper along with the words "For Miss Thompson. From Teddy."

All the children watched as the teacher open the gift. As she removed the last bit of tape, a gaudy rhinestone bracelet and a small, half-empty bottle of cologne fell to the desk. Several children snickered and began whispering.

Unable to look at Teddy, the teacher picked up the bracelet and said, "Oh, how lovely." She asked if Teddy would help her fasten it on her wrist.

When she dabbed the perfume behind her ears, the girls lined up for a dab too.

The Christmas party ended and all the children left the room, but Teddy waited at his desk. When he was alone with the teacher, he walked toward her and said, "You smell just like Mom. Her bracelet looks real pretty on you too. I'm glad you like it." Then he left quickly. The teacher sat at her desk in silence, tears in her eyes, reflecting on how limited her concern for Teddy had been.

Parents Can Model the Self-Discipline Skills

Teachers are always grateful when parents support the expectations they have established in the school. Parents can model the following self-discipline skills.

FOLLOWING INSTRUCTIONS: Follow the school procedures for pick up and drop off of students.

SHARING SPACE: Monitor pre-school children and insist they hold your hand and not let them run freely through the school building.

INDEPENDENTLY COMPLETE TASKS: Teach students to be responsible for their belongings – coats, sweaters, hats, etc. and ask them to search the lost and found if something is not returned to the home.

INDEPENDENTLY COMPLETE TASKS: Allow children to take the natural consequence for their actions. They refuse to bring forgotten items to the school but do coach students on productive ways to get ready for school.

COMMUICATION: Use an appropriate voice tone when meeting with teachers and ask if they need to make an appointment.

ORGANIZATION: When volunteering for a school activity, parents ask for a check-list of expected duties. They follow the expectations and offer feedback regarding student performance.

CHAPTER 8

Exhibiting Social Skills

 Mastering simple social skills enables us to be accepted and live among others in harmony. It also enables us to be receptive to others and their thoughts and ideas. This drawing illustrates and connectedness and interdependence of various kinds of lines to form art.

When we use SOCIAL SKILLS,

We WAIT until we have noticed another person;

We THINK: How can I make this person feel comfortable or at ease?

We ACT: We greet the other person or introduce ourselves.

Social Skills and Expectations

William McKinley, the 25th U.S. president, once had to choose between two equally qualified men for a key job. He puzzled over the candidates until he remembered an incident one rainy night aboard a crowded streetcar. One of the men he was now considering for employment had also boarded, although he hadn't seen McKinley. In the streetcar, an old woman carrying a basket of laundry struggled in, looking in vain for a seat. The job candidate pretended not to see her and kept his seat. As she moved further down the aisle, McKinley gave her his seat. Remembering the episode, which he called "a little omission of kindness," McKinley decided against the man for the job (Boller, 1981).

What others notice about us when we first meet is our use or lack of social skills. Do we appear friendly or stand-offish? Do we know how to greet others and show by our facial expressions that we are willing to engage in conversation? Our social interactions convey much about our character.

Social skills are rules that help people relate to one another in a positive manner. People who know social expectations will feel comfortable in diverse social settings. Today, we cannot assume uniformity in social skills unless they become a part of school and home cultures. What is acceptable in one family may not be tolerated in another. Consequently, teachers must identify and encourage the practice of basic social skills to develop a civilized classroom culture. Where no common norms exist, the 15 skills can become the norm, regardless of culture/ethnic groupings.

Social Skills in Children Birth to Five

On a rerun of the reality show *Nanny 911*, I noted screaming children and disorder throughout the household. Defiant little mouths shouted, "No. I hate you! You can't make me do it," to parents who seemed helpless to react, unwilling or unable to set limits and take a firm stand against such behavior. The nanny observed patterns of behaviors that were unproductive and looked beyond the words spoken. Her message was that the children needed a parent's time, love, and concern. They needed adults to set limits on screen watching, video games, rough-housing, and offensive words. The children needed parents capable of putting aside their own needs, to establish routines and consistency to build a safe and comfortable environment.

The nanny outlined a daily schedule including mealtimes, chores, free time, and productive play. Establishing new routines took thought and planning. Parents had to stick to the new routine for three weeks to convince children of its permanence. Children experienced attention and connections with their parents and their groaning and complaining eventually ceased.

Before someone can engage in social interaction, they have to notice others. Beyond that, they must learn to empathize, to imagine how someone else is feeling, and respond appropriately. Developmental phases lead to a child's readiness to learn social skills. As early as six months, babies take cues from their parents regarding reactions to new people. When parents are warm and welcoming, it can influence how the baby responds. By 20 months, most young children recognize themselves in a mirror as a distinct and separate person. This milestone allows parents and teachers to talk about how another person might feel. When parents describe a person's face as registering happiness or sadness, they nurture empathy in their toddler.

Many a parent has said, "Don't forget to say thank you; "How do we greet someone?" and, "Remember to wash your hands." By the time children are school age, teachers see gaps in the social etiquette of young children. Independent companies now offer classes on table manners and social skills because parents and businesses recognize the value of social skills in our culture.

Social Skills in Primary Grades

Much of a primary teacher's time revolves around social skills. Teachers help the little ones learn to moderate their voices, use greeting and leaving skills, make introductions, use polite words, and learn the difference between helpful and hurtful messages. Teachers attend to hygiene, dress, moods, tears, and fights.

Children learn to say "Thank you" when:

Someone gives you something.
Someone does something for you.
Someone compliments you.

There are four times when "Excuse me" is the appropriate response:

1. When you need to interrupt.
2. When you need someone to move out of the way.
3. When you make an impolite sound (one that could be offensive to another person).
4. When you must leave the table.

When saying "Thank you" or "Excuse me" is intentionally taught, children self-monitor each time they use these phrases and can earn tokens, prizes, or time with an adult.

Tattling

Tattling, a developmental trait in kindergarten through third grade, can be viewed negatively or thought of in terms of skill development. Up until third grade, many children do not understand Skill #7 – Reason for the Rules; however, they feel a moral obligation to report to an adult when they perceive a rule to be broken. You can tell if a child just needs to report if they run off happily when you say, "Thank you for telling me."

Another way to validate children's need to report is to cover a shoe box and label it Tattle Box, I Witness Box, or Observation Box. Near the box, place small pieces of paper and a crayon or pencil and encourage children to draw or write what they see or hear. An adult can promise to read the entries anonymously once a week to the class. This way, the adult can bring up topics of concern without singling out specific students and meet with those students privately. They can also highlight good comments to encourage more positive peer reporting.

Older children often tattle to get another person in trouble or get help with a problem they do not know how to fix. In these cases, the teacher can encourage students to think about the question, "Am I tattling to help or hurt someone?" This can lead to discussion and appropriate action. Teach children the difference between reporting dangerous, immoral, or illegal activities and tattling.

Sometimes, a student's apparent lack of social skills reflects the inability to demonstrate a higher-level skill. Children may not have learned words to communicate their thoughts. They may be unable to separate facts from feelings; therefore, they react emotionally to situations. Sometimes, words that are unacceptable to use at school are acceptable in the children's family or community. *DWP* teachers emphasize social skills as behaviors people agree upon, to live harmoniously with others. They instruct students to avoid words or gestures that may make even one person uncomfortable.

Gestures and body language give clues to what a person might be thinking or feeling. Popular or quick one-word answers such as "Whatever" or "So?" stop communication. Teachers of *DWP* ask learners to describe in a sentence or two what such dismissive language might mean to a listener. Since these words are often used as shortcuts, learners can design signs that read "No Shortcuts" and place them in areas around the school where the use of these words and expressions should be avoided.

What adults perceive to be mean behavior by children is also an opportunity to civilize and enculturate children into the adult world. These spontaneous responses or habits require training to manage impulse control.

Table Etiquette

One summer, my nine-year-old niece came from Maryland to visit me in Nebraska. During her two-week stay, I planned many activities to help her enjoy her visit. One afternoon, as the two of us were lunching in a restaurant that wasn't fast food, Carla whispered across the table, "Aunt Barb, what did you do with your napkin?" I said, "I put it on my lap. Perplexed, Carla replied, "I didn't know what to do with it, so I left it by my plate." Quite sure that Carla's mother would have taught table manners, I asked her, "What do you do when you are at home?" Carla replied, "With the seven of us in the family, I think mom thinks napkins are too expensive. She just passes a towel around."

Table etiquette usually learned at the family dinner table, can be practiced at the school lunch table and at home. Here are some guidelines:

Silence cell phones.
Unfold your napkin and place it in your lap before you start eating.
Once you touch a piece of food, put it on your plate.
Do not reach across the table for something. Say, "Please pass the _____."
Chew with your mouth closed and do not speak with food in your mouth.
Talk quietly with the people seated near you. Take turns talking.
Say "Excuse me" when you must leave the table.
Keep your elbows off the table.
When you are done eating, fold your napkin and lay it on the table.

Use Poetry to Highlight the Skill

No Napkin in My Lunch
By Christine Ryktarsyk

There's one thing that bugs me.
It bothers me a bunch.
It's when I first discover
There's no napkin in my lunch.

I reach behind the sandwich.
I look behind my pear.
I search the whole darn lunchbox...
But the napkin isn't there.

I'm usually quite hungry.
When it's time, I dive right in.
Wish I knew about the napkin
Before the pudding on my chin.

Then I feel embarrassed...
I don't know what to do.
Next time, I'll find my napkin
Before I start to chew.

All my friends are eating
Very neatly, full of grace.
While I search for my napkin
With my food upon my face.

Social Skills in Grades Four through Eight

The word "etiquette" derives from the French royal courts in the 1600 and 1700s. It was later expanded to describe expected behavior of knights. Tickets were issued for right conduct and listed the expected ways of behavior befitting a knight. One ticket might describe how to help a lady in distress, while another might tell of proper manners when dining at the king's table. Always, etiquette put others at ease and was based on custom or tradition, consideration for others, and common sense.

Students in grades four through eight learn to use the three C's – custom, courtesy, and common sense – to determine appropriate actions. Custom, pertaining to the past, is framed by three questions: Is there a custom or tradition of proper behavior? Can I honor it? Should I change or modify it? Courtesy pertains to the present: In this situation, what would I like someone to do for me? Common sense pertains to the future: What would happen if no one acted this way? What would happen if everyone acted this way?

My sister and brother-in-law have seven married children. They have delighted in watching their twenty-two grandchildren, ranging in ages from two to eighteen. They have resolved not to interfere with the children and spouses' different parenting styles, though they are aware of social skills present or lacking. In one family, for example, all the children have been trained to take their plates over to the sink when they are finished eating. In another, thank you notes are always sent after receiving gifts. In a third, the children spontaneously greet them with words and hugs. They also notice when children are unable to focus on a family meal and remain at the table until everyone is finished. Others readily interrupt adult conversations. When some children received gifts not to their liking, they pout and talk about the gift they had expected.

One Christmas, they decided to teach the grandchildren the appropriate way to say, "Thank you," using the acronym *NET-1* to teach proper behavior when receiving a gift:

Say the person's *name*
Look the person in the *eye*
Tell the person, *"Thank you."*
Say at least *one* thing you like.

Example: Look your aunt in the eye and say, "Aunt Carolyn, thank you! I love the color of this sweater and it feels so soft." When children skipped a step, the grandparents coached them: "How about the E?" or "How about the N?"

The grandparents discovered the impact of their teaching a few months later when grandpa received gifts for his birthday. While opening his first gift, one of the grandchildren remarked, "Grandpa, don't forget about *Net-1*."

Bullying: A Negative Social Skill

Bullying is a negative social skill. Bullies derive pleasure when their victim cowers, cries, or shows fear or intimidation. Bullies deliberately choose to exclude others. American culture has learned to embrace hazing activities that humiliate, degrade, abuse, and even endanger the person initiated into a group. The problem of bullying is cultural and multi-dimensional. Without reflection, anyone could be a bully.

Most, if not all schools, have an Anti-Bully program, designed to help when behavior occurs repeatedly over time, which the victim describes as an ongoing pattern of harassment or abuse. In the age of social media, bullying has taken on a new perspective. There are five types of bullies:

Physical Bullies – Enjoy taking or damaging their target's property.

Relational Bullies – Convince peers to reject someone from their group.

Verbal Bullies – Leave scars that may not be visible but are more painful emotionally and last longer than bruises.

Reactive Bullies – Have been bullied and finally strike out at their attackers.

Cyber Bullies – Inflict willful and repeated harm through the social networks, interactive technologies, or mobile phones through harassing, humiliating, or threatening text or images. Cyberbullies are often difficult to track; consequently, the posted pictures, gossip, and false stories can be extremely damaging.

The use of the Internet, to make friends and network, presents unique etiquette challenges. Anything posted on the Internet has the potential of going viral. These new communication tools can be detrimental as well as beneficial. When the effects are detrimental, there are strategies parents can use to help discourage bullying:

- Create a culture in the home where meanness is not tolerated. Teach kindness, empathy, caring, and giving.
- Have boundaries and discipline children without using abusive or excessive punishment.
- Discourage hitting, pushing, and teasing.
- Encourage children to talk to you about bullies and bullying.
- Don't encourage children to fight a bully. Suggest walking away or seeking help from an adult. Help them practice saying, "Stop that," or, "If you don't stop, I will report this."
- Tell your children you're responsible for protecting them. Without promising secrecy, tell them that you'll work out a plan to inform the school in a way that doesn't worsen the abuse.
- Use the guidelines the school has for reporting bullying.

- Don't wait to seek treatment for a depressed child. Bullies and victims may need treatment for depression.
- Normalize conversation about school social life. Instead of asking, "How was school today?" ask, "Who did you have lunch with?"; "Who did you play with?"; "Do you ever notice kids being teased or picked on or excluded?"
- Monitor your child's Internet activity to ensure they are using proper etiquette. If your child is being cyber-bullied, report it (Volpitta & Haber 2012).

> "When we are skilled in managing our relationships, we are more likely to build and maintain a network of support. Far from being just a matter of good form, civility is also a matter of good health."
>
> Choosing Civility, P.M. Forni, p. 30

Bess Introduces a Speaker

The following dialogue took place between an eighth grader and a teacher during a lunch break. The teacher employed an intervention known as pre-teaching, which reviews details of an activity before it happens.

Teacher: "Bess, I know you will be introducing Mr. Welsh to our class on Thursday, and I was wondering if you have ever introduced a speaker before.

Bess: "No."

Teacher: "Well, I'd like to review with you how other people introduce speakers. Do you have time to do this now?"

Bess: "Sure."

Teacher: "Let's picture this. Where did you tell Mr. Welsh you would meet him?"

Bess: "I told him to meet me at the school office."

Teacher: "When you meet Mr. Welsh, it will be expected that you introduce yourself and get his full name to make sure you are bringing the right person down to our room. Have you thought about how you will do this?"

Bess: "I'll say, 'Hi, my name is Bess.'"

Teacher: "In our culture it is appropriate to reach out your hand and shake his as you give both your first and last names. From the office to our classroom, what will you talk about?"

Bess: "I thought I would talk with Mr. Welsh about my uncle who works with him."

Teacher: "That's great! Networking is always important. If Mr. Welsh hasn't met Principal Grey, you might introduce him since you will pass right by his office."

Bess: "I never thought of that."

Teacher: "When you get to the classroom, how will he want the room arranged? Will he bring a resume for you to use? Is there something specific he will want you to say about him?"

Bess: "I'd better write some of these things down."

At the appointed time, Bess brought Mr. Welsh to her classroom. She used the short biographical sketch Mr. Welsh provided and had the room arranged as he suggested. The following day, on her own initiative, she brought to class a thank-you card and invited everyone to sign it. When the teacher phoned Mr. Welsh to discover his impression of the class activity, he was extremely complementary of Bess's ability to cooperate with all his requests. She had successfully used her social skills and the wait, think, act process.

CHAPTER 9

Teaching the Constructive Skills

```
THE CONSTRUCTIVE SKILLS
Coached – Birth to Grade Three
Optimum time to teach: Grade Three – Grade Six

     6.  Cooperating
     7.  Understanding the Reasons for Rules
     8.  Independently Accomplish Tasks
     9.  Exhibiting Leadership
     10. Communicating Effectively
```

Setting the Stage

The school principal visited a fifth-grade classroom at the beginning of the school year to tell the students she had high hopes for them. She hoped they would enjoy learning all the new subjects they would be taught, that they would get along with one another and enjoy their year. Most of all, she hoped they would learn how to become more self-disciplined. Becoming self-disciplined for fifth graders means they can demonstrate the five Basic self-discipline skills. It also means they must try their hardest during the fifth-grade year to practice the five Constructive skills.

The principal moved to the board, listed, and explained each of the Constructive Skills. She expected students to cooperate with others, learn and follow the rules of the school and classroom, and take on leadership roles. She wanted them to learn new ways to accomplish tasks, even if it their ways differed from everyone else. Finally, she hoped they would develop better communication skills, learn to disagree appropriately, and voice opinions respectfully.

The principal said, "I know many things have happened to each one of you over the summer. Some were pleasant events and some not so pleasant. You are not the same persons you were last year when you were in the fourth grade. I expect you to let one another change and be different. I'm asking you to give yourselves permission to start over and make this school year one of the best."

When the principal finished, one young man asked if he could make a copy of the new skills. "I always wanted to be self-disciplined," he said. "I just never knew how to get there."

The Constructive Skills: Grades Three through Six

The Constructive Skills build on the five Basic Skills. These five skills form the foundation for solving problems in a democratic manner. Students learn to:

- Develop techniques to work with others: (Cooperation)
- Create procedures that outline how rules will be followed: (Understanding Rules)
- Make independent decisions concerning homework and class projects: (Independently Complete Tasks)
- Write speeches to defend pro or con positions (Communication): and,
- Accept positions of leadership (Exhibiting Leadership)

Students are taught that everyone has a right to voice their opinion if words are spoken in a respectful manner. Problems can be solved in a democratic manner when the Constructive Skills are acknowledged as essential in a civil society. Without these skills, people fail to enter into the democratic process and exercise their rights and responsibilities as citizens.

The focus of the Constructive Skills is primarily on rights, responsibilities, and active participation. We teach these skills so children learn they are contributors to the social good rather than beings who simply abide by the rules. In learning these skills, they can exchange ideas and work with other children to achieve mutually understood goals. Participating in curriculum planning, choosing projects, and voicing an opinion all require higher level cognitive processes. We teach these skills so children recognize the needs and rights of others and the effects of their action on others. Understanding the concept of justice, and the ideal of respect for every individual, is embedded in the Constructive Skills (Tanner, p. 32-33).

As you read about individual Constructive Skills, notice how the skills overlap and intersect. The main benchmarks of the Constructive Skills are on learning how to work with other people, thinking critically and independently, and evaluating the choices that are made.

Describe the Constructive Skills in Terms of 'Growing Up'

By the end of third grade, referring to self-discipline skills as 'hidden skills' no longer captures the attention of the growing child. Many fourth graders begin to think of themselves as miniature adults. In some ways, the personality they now have will continue into adulthood. This is the perfect time to capitalize on the concept of 'growing-up' as a motivator to practice the skills. They can learn growing up may have less to do with age and more to do with acquiring the skills of self-discipline needed for a lifetime. As they begin the skills program, students are asked questions such as:

- What will you be able to do as a grown up that you are not able to do now?
- At what age do you think you will be grown up?
- Is it possible to practice being a grown up at your age?
- What would you do?
- Has anyone ever shared with you the tasks you will need to learn before you can be considered grown up?

When the fifth graders were asked, "What will you be able to do as a grown up?" they responded that they will be able to drive, drink, and carry credit cards, have a family, build a house, work, and vote. Few students thought about growing up in terms of getting themselves ready emotionally, socially, intellectually, and morally through skill development. To support the concept that growing up relates to skill development and to make the concept more relational, we shared the following anecdotes.

I have a friend who is 40 years old, six feet tall, and who has a good job, wife, and family, but does not consider himself to be "grown up." If you asked my friend why he doesn't think he is grown up, he would describe a lack of self-discipline skills. "Just ask my wife. She will tell you that I start projects around the house but never finish them. I get stuck and can't figure out how to accomplish a task. I don't like asking for help." My friend believes if he wants to grow-up, he should begin practicing these missing skills.

I also told the students about my 12-year-old niece who was proud she had asked a question in Math class. Math was difficult for her, so she decided to begin with one good question, with the goal of asking three questions by the end of the week. When asked why she was proud of this action, she promptly stated, "Because asking questions is a skill I need for the rest of my life and I want to start practicing it now."

After this discussion, one student privately told me, "When I looked at the skills, I realized that my mother practices all of them, but my dad doesn't do many at all. My parents are divorced. My dad looks at me when he speaks but he doesn't really hear what I am saying. He doesn't organize his time and is often late when he picks me up."

I started to give the student words of encouragement when he stopped me. "Oh, there is a lot of hope for my dad," he said. "Our school sent home a list of the self-discipline skills and my dad has them on his refrigerator. He is already starting to practice them."

What a healthy way to think about a situation that might have left the boy wondering if he was to blame for the divorce. He seemed to have grasped the concept that the only person you can change is yourself, and no one can do the work of growing up for anyone else.

Be mindful that some students may not want to grow up. Experience has taught them that too much responsibility comes with this title. Be sensitive to this issue. After an initial discussion, refer to skills six through ten as the Constructive Skills and help students discover how they build on skills one to five.

Motivating Students to Practice Self-Discipline

To ensure that all skills are taught at least once during a year, teachers post the 15 skills face down across the front of the classroom. On the back of each poster, one letter, and the hyphen in "self-discipline" is printed. Every three weeks, a student selects a letter and reveals a skill. The following day, a lesson is taught about each skill. Students record the information in their skills booklets or journals. During the remainder of the three weeks, students set personal goals to practice each.

Students in grades four to six build skill bracelets or necklaces of colored beads. Each bead represents a different skill. When three adults in the community witness a student practicing the featured skill, and initial their personal skill card, the student can acquire a bead. Bracelets and necklaces continue to be created throughout the school year.

Students are assigned homework to interview adults and ask the following survey questions:

- What do you most like about being grown-up?
- What is challenging for you as a grown-up?
- What skills are easy for you and difficult for you to practice? Why?
- Which of the skills benefit adults the most? Why?

Teaching Constructive Skills in Kindergarten through Third Grade

When the entire 15-skills framework is used in every grade, teachers can infuse skill vocabulary at teachable moments. Identifying a primary child as a leader or communicator sets the stage for students to learn more fully about these skills in later grades. Teachers can infuse the five Constructive skills into their existing curriculum. Grade-level literature will highlight certain skills and *Discipline with Purpose* lesson plans include stories of animals that exhibit the skills. Here are some examples:

Carla the Cooperating Cow: Cows cooperate by looking out for the old and weak members in a herd. When dairy cows return to be milked, a leader is selected to guide the way. The older or weaker cows are helped along by the stronger ones. If a cow in a herd is shocked by an electric fence, the rest of the herd will become alarmed and learn to avoid the fence. Students are given a picture of Carla to paste in their skills booklet and label the picture – "We cooperate like Carla when we work together as a class."

Rosco the Rambunctious Rabbit: The Rabbit runs off the school grounds and on to people's lawns in hunt of four-leaf clovers. He digs up the students' garden and, during the Easter egg hunt, Rosco runs through the school yard to gather eggs before the students can get them. Rosco is helped by a loving high school student who explains the rules to him and gives him reasons for obeying the rules. Students must identify what the high school student told Rosco to do to obey the rules when he was outside. They paste a picture of Rosco in their skills booklet and list three playground rules:

- Play quietly so others are not disturbed.
- Stay with your class and don't leave the school grounds without permission.
- Respect other people's things. Don't take what doesn't belong to you.

Freddy the Fish Who Finishes Everything: Students talk about some things the fish might need to do every day, such as find food, protect themselves from predators, and swim. Students then think of actions they must do by themselves every day and draw pictures in their skills booklet.

Leroy the Leading Lion: Two types of lions, the African and the Asiatic lion, are presented. Leroy, the fully-grown male lion left his family and took over a group of other lions. As a leader he had to defend his territory. Leroy was known for his courage and strength. Students explore what leaders do for the class.

Sally the Smooth-talking Skunk: The students learn that skunks hunt for food at night. They eat fruit and plants, insects, worms, eggs, reptiles, and fish. Skunks are known for spraying a horrible-smelling oily liquid that chases people away. The spray causes no real damage, but it makes people feel uncomfortable and the smell can stay around for many days. The illustration of Sally as a smooth-talking skunk is a joke. Sally shows by her actions she does not want to communicate or be around others. Students discuss the fact that sometimes people say or do things that make others feel uncomfortable.

CHAPTER 10

The Skill of Cooperating

 As in weaving, we are uniquely pulled from many strands. When woven together, we work to create a cloth of humanity, the common good.

When we COOPERATE:

We WAIT for everyone to complete their portions of a task.

We THINK: Do I need to ask for help from a peer? Can I help anyone else? What will make all members of our team winners?

We ACT: We complete our portion of a task to the best of our abilities.

About ten years ago in Stockholm, Sweden, unemployable young people, ages 18 to 25, were assigned to teams and given the opportunity to write, direct, produce, shoot, and act in their own original films. Two requirements for membership were no drug taking/selling or involvement in crime as a gang member. The typical participant tended to think of short-term gratification rather than long-term goals. Participants had little self-discipline, were extremely reactive to circumstances, and did not generally accept responsibility for their actions.

As the teams worked together, many learned to use the 15 self-discipline skills to finish the task. Participants had to listen to one another, learn how to brainstorm, creatively solve problems, initiate solutions, report to class on time, and finish assigned tasks. They had to effectively communicate their ideas to an audience and establish their own timelines. The filmmaking process required them to deal with complexity. It changed their focus from the subjective (how things feel) to the objective (what reality is, no matter how you feel). They began to think in terms of relationships. How do things fit together? How can something filmed on one day match something filmed many days later? How can the end resolve the dramatic conflicts that had been set up in the beginning of the story?

Joining together for a common purpose and vision taught the participants how to support rather than compete with one another. One of the biggest changes in the participants was their shift from impulsive (I don't feel like getting out of bed today) to self-disciplined behavior.

During their time together, all participants had to come up with at least one major goal for their lives. Life coaches were available to help the students make their goals a reality. Some participants went back to school; others learned how to manage finances. Still others learned how to avoid pitfalls that led to dead ends and establish healthy relationships. Learning the principles of the creative process helped some of the most disadvantaged members of society transform into productive contributors. This success is instructive for *DWP* educators, who often ask the following reflective questions:

- How do we encourage the creative process?
- Do we provide students with clear limits so they can safely explore ideas and activities?
- Do we set high standards and then help students to meet those standards?
- Do we encourage collaboration and cooperation rather than independence and competition?
- Do we connect the practice of self-discipline skills with success in life?

What Does It Mean to Cooperate?

The skill of cooperation is taught to build group cohesiveness and learn how to work productively with theirs. In the process, strengths and weaknesses can be individually identified, unproductive group activities can be eliminated, and members can learn strategies for group decision making. Cooperation means to act or work with others for mutual benefit.

Unlike the skill of sharing – working side by side doing the same task – cooperation usually involves a different action for each person in the group. Children practice cooperation when they are members of a sports team, play in an orchestra, belong to a dance troop, or act in a theater production. Adults cooperate at work, in the home, and when building relationships.

Why Cooperating May Be a Challenging Skill

As a rule, the ability to cooperate with three or more persons will be difficult for children in third through sixth grade. Some middle grade students have difficulty with cooperation as well. We asked middle grade students to give reasons why students fail to work well together. They told us that some students don't care about other people. They may be very bright and prefer to work alone. Some students don't think the task is important, and some simply don't know how to cooperate. Others don't want to be criticized if they don't do their part of the task right.

A closer look at children of this age reveals why cooperation and the other constructive skills are developmentally difficult. Between third and sixth grade, children notice inequities in privileges and inconsistencies in the actions of parents and teachers. They believe rules have exceptions and can be modified. They start to question motives and note that circumstances change matters. If an action is an accident, children expect that the consequence will differ from that of an action purposefully done. A limited vocabulary and/or communication skill causes them to express themselves inappropriately. The focus is often on the quick fix, which leaves the quality of their work questionable. When adults recognize and appreciate these innate tendencies, the need to develop the constructive self-discipline skills becomes more evident.

Regarding cooperative skills, Dr. Tanner writes:

> While some cooperative activities fail, because learners lack the necessary skills and attitudes, others fail for a different reason: the nature of the activity. If children are to learn to work together on a common problem, it must be a real problem which gives them real social responsibility. Children learn by taking part in what is going on according to their developing abilities. Many small group activities fail because the problems seem contrived to the children. The curriculum must allow the children to function in real situations,

not just discuss them. They must act to accomplish an objective that they have arrived at in concert with others (1978, p. 34).

Three Essential Elements of Cooperation

The most obvious requirement in a cooperative effort is knowing the names and something about each team member. Group members can interview one another using designated questions. A team can develop a list of questions they would like all members to answer. Group members can write two true and one untrue statement about themselves. As each person shares what they have written, team members can ask questions to discern the false statement. Once team members become familiar with one another, there are three essential elements and two guiding principles to the skill of cooperation. The two key principles operative in cooperation are:

- group members can ask for help.
- group members can offer to help others in need.

The three essential elements are as follows:

1. **Identify individual tasks and a group goal.** Group members realize that achieving the goal requires everyone to do their share of the work. Imagine breaking a completed 100-piece puzzle into five sections. Each section is broken into 20 pieces and placed in a plastic bag. Five students are each given one of the bags with the goal of putting the puzzle back together. In this exercise the task is clear, the group goal, assembling the puzzle, needs everyone's participation.

2. **Develop a support system.** Group members work as a support system. They learn to interact in positive ways to encourage, explain, and teach one another. They recognize members who offer to help others. They review group interactions that were helpful and those that were less productive. They look for each person's strengths and leadership qualities. They learn from one another as the tasks rotate.

3. **Evaluate individual and group efforts.** Two evaluations are needed when the goal is reached. One evaluation measures the success of the group project and one measures individual member's efforts.

Reflection questions include: 1) Was the puzzle able to be completed in the time allotted?; 2) Did each person complete their section independently or with help?; 3) On a scale of one to five, low to high, choose the number that represents both the individual and group effort to complete the goal.

Brainstorming

Brainstorming, a technique that usually lasts five to ten minutes can help people feel they are part of the group process. As individual members of the group generate ideas, they are recorded. Ideas can be realistic or fanciful. No judgment is passed on the value of each suggestion until the end of the brainstorming session, when the pros and cons of each idea is discussed. Reasons are given for eliminating as well as keeping the suggestions listed. The ideas that help move the group to the desired goal are recorded and then voted upon. The most essential element when brainstorming is the absence of criticism and negative comments. The following guidelines are used when brainstorming:

All ideas are significant and should be recorded.
Everyone can have equal time to explain an idea.
The ideas will be evaluated according to established criteria: reasonableness, time, cost, et cetera.
The group must come to a consensus on the idea to be selected.
The best idea incorporates many different points of view.

For adults, there is disagreement over which process generates a diverse set of ideas: working as individuals or brainstorming with a group. Leigh Thompson, a professor at the Kellogg School of Management at Northwestern University, performed extensive research on brainstorming and found that individuals are better at thinking broadly to generate a diverse set of ideas, while groups are better at selecting which goals or ideas are worth pursuing.

Cooperating in School

In school, when cooperative learning groups are utilized, each member of the group will be assigned a different task. According to the age of the children and the number of groups members, individual roles are defined and rotate. A Reader will scan all printed information and assign group work as needed. A Materials Manager will obtain necessary supplies and keep all group work together for future planning sessions. A Recorder may write down important information. A Researcher will be charged with locating information. The Reporter will give the oral report and a Monitor may hand out tickets to members of the group who disrupt the cooperative efforts.

In the primary grades, to highlight when cooperation is needed, *DWP* teachers sing the Cooperation Song created by Jo Mersnick and sung to the tune of *When Johnny Comes Marching Home*.

The Cooperation Song

When there is a job that we must do, Cooperate.
Make up a plan and work it through, Cooperate.
Agree and delegate,
Talk and plan,
Work together and say, "We can!" and
We'll get the job done
When we all Cooperate.
Remember evaluate.
When finished we'll celebrate.

Cooperation at Home

In Chapter 11, we suggest that parents adopt rules similar to school rules. One rule is to contribute to the household. Parents often say, "My child is really good in school, but when he comes home, he's a different person." The parents say their child doesn't follow instructions, bothers siblings, has a messy room, and generally does not contribute to the household. Of course, I always ask what expectations and responsibilities the child is assigned at home. Some parents think there is too much pressure on children today; they don't want to give them added responsibilities.

In other cases, I find children have been expected to take on tasks that rightfully belong to the adults. For example, some are responsible for the care of younger siblings, provide meals, or take care of the parent's emotional needs. In healthy families, everyone contributes to the welfare and functioning of the family unit.

Children are given tasks appropriate to their age. Here is an example of a list for a ten-year-old, who receives age-appropriate chores.

1. Dress yourself.
2. Brush your teeth.
3. Pick clothes up off the floor.
4. Feed the pet.
5. Put dirty dishes in the sink or dishwasher.
6. Finish all homework.
7. Show your finished work to a parent.
8. Without their asking, report to a parent three things you learned in school.
9. Once a day, ask if there is anything you can do to help the family.
10. Do something nice for a family member.

Routine jobs such as taking out the trash or feeding the family pet rotate and are the parents' as well as the children's responsibility. Parents help children cooperate by indicating, on a weekly/monthly calendar, the times and places where individuals need to be. Family members check the calendar periodically to be sure there are not too many activities taking away from family time. They discuss the importance of everyone in the family contributing to the household.

Cooperation Requires the Use of Many Self-Discipline Skills

Cooperation requires the use of a combination of self-discipline skills. Foremost is the skill of listening. Students learn how to compliment and encourage group members. The ability to independently complete tasks and problem solve are also cooperation skills. Managing conflict is important when building teamwork. Simple strategies for conflict resolution with primary students include rock-paper-scissors, thumbs-up or thumbs-down, and flipping a coin. More complex strategies include learning how to accommodate, collaborate, and compromise (See Chapter 17).

Practicing the skill of cooperation may seem awkward to students at first. Learning the correct words to say when negotiating or complimenting a teammate can feel inauthentic. Learning to wait to avoid making negative or positive comments during brainstorming, can feel uncomfortable. Practice is needed until the skill occurs naturally.

> "By treating you the best way I know how, I appeal to the best in you, urging you to do the same. The practice of civility is the applying of gentle force with the goal that everybody be a winner in the delicate game of the social exchange."
>
> Choosing Civility, P.M. Forni, p. 27

Bo Practices a New Skill

Bo was a sixth grader. He was in a school that had taught the 15 self-discipline skills for four years. On one day, the youngsters were to name one skill they felt they had mastered and one that was a challenge for them. Bo told the class how asking questions was an easy skill, but cooperation was difficult. "I don't cooperate at home and I don't cooperate at school," he said. His classmates nodded in agreement.

The teacher thanked Bo for sharing that information and calmly encouraged him: "Cooperation is a difficult skill for some people to acquire without help. I don't know when or if you will decide to practice the skill. I hope it will be sometime soon, because you will need this skill the rest of your life." Bo accepted the comment without retort. A short time later, the class received an assignment and the teacher noticed that Bo was the first one finished. "Would you please pick up the papers as your classmates finish the assignment?" the teacher asked of him. Bo moved quietly around the room, picking up the completed papers. When he was finished, he sorted the papers so all the headings were top side up. When the papers were perfect, Bo handed the completed stack to his teacher.

"Oh, Bo," the teacher said emphatically. "About 20 minutes ago you told us that cooperation was a difficult skill for you to do, but just now, by your actions, you showed us what that skill looks like." Several of Bo's classmates overheard the comment and spontaneously began to clap. "Bo just practiced cooperation!" one of them said. With that, the entire class gave Bo a round of applause.

Bo learned an important lesson – that people will be good at some skills and not so good at others. When he wants to improve, he'll just have to practice.

CHAPTER 11

The Skill of Understanding and Following Rules

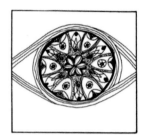

Mastering the skill of understanding rules and the reasons for rules shows a kind of wisdom. This drawing is based on the 15th century Islamic symbol for wisdom – the almond-shaped mandala or eye of wisdom. It is also a reference to the old saying, "The eyes are the window to the soul."

When we UNDERSTAND THE REASONS FOR RULES AND FOLLOW THEM,

We WAIT to learn what rules have already been made.

We THINK: Do I know the reason for the rule? Who can I ask if I do not understand why the rule was made?

We ACT: We follow the rule or work to change it.

While most of the *Discipline with Purpose* schools are kindergarten through ninth grade, some private high schools have adopted the skills framework. V.J. and Angela Skutt Catholic High School in Omaha, Nebraska, offers a year-long character skills class incorporating the 15 self-discipline skills. The following exchange took place between the skills teacher and Michaela, a sophomore:

Teacher: "Which of the 15 self-discipline skills comes into play most often in the life of a teenager?"

Sophomore: "All the skills are used every day, but I find skill seven challenging… Understanding Rules and the Reasons for Rules."

Teacher: "What do you find challenging about this skill?"

Sophomore: "Sometimes adults make rules or tell us about the rules of society and then expect that once the words have been spoken, it is now a law. It makes me feel like I want to go against the rule to see if it really needs to be there. Sometimes I don't really understand the reasons behind some of the rules and when a rule is just stated without giving the reason it makes me feel like an order was given by a boss who won't let me have control in the matter."

Teacher: "How has your idea about this skill changed from grade school to high school?"

Sophomore: "As a member of student council, I am actually involved in making some of the rules for activities. We must listen to different points of view before arriving at suggestions or procedures that we will ask everyone to follow. This helps me understand what makes an effective rule. In addition, I have gone against rules in past years and each time I make bad decisions or mistakes, it helps me to better understand the reasons behind the rule. For example: I was told not to go to the mall alone when I was younger. Once I went on my own and witnessed a fight. It scared me and I began to see one reason why parents didn't want me to go alone."

Teacher: "Have you had any opportunities to actually change a rule?"

Sophomore: "Yes, as a member of the cheerleading squad, I went with other students to request permission to have the number of pep rallies increased so we could get more school spirit going. We listed our reasons for the request and asked that the matter be taken into advisement. We were able to increase the number of pep rallies."

Teacher: "In your opinion, how can adults help students in middle school and junior high learn to practice this skill better?"

Sophomore: "There are three things that help me learn about rules and the reasons for rules: 1) When adults talk to me in a calm voice and not make demands or scare me into following a rule; 2) When they tell me why the rule is a good one, give examples, or talk about examples from life or in the newspaper; 3) When they tell me beforehand what the consequence will be if the rule is not followed."

In this conversation, the teacher highlighted the fact that school rules are not just a poster hanging on a wall or mandates issued by adults. The rules are living documents reviewed and changed when they no longer serve a purpose. They are a benefit to all members of the community, and all can take ownership by evaluating their effectiveness.

Rules, Procedures, and Skills

Civilizations have learned much by studying the inherent laws found in nature. No society ever achieved greatness without realizing the importance of rules. No person ever became great without defining their own limits. No skill is more essential for a civilized community than having members of the community understand the rules and their reasons. Yet, sometimes we perceive rules as obstacles, not opportunities. "When we teach the reason for rules, we are trying to develop a sense of responsibility and consideration for others, coupled with the understanding that rules are for the purpose of making classroom life pleasant, productive and possible" (Tanner, p. 30-31).

The word "rule" comes from the Latin "regere," which is defined as "to lead straight." Rules are a prescribed guide for conduct or action or a standard of judgment. The word "procedure" comes from the Latin "procedere," which means "to go forward." Procedures refer to an established way of doing things. When the absence of a standard operating procedure (SOP) compromises the existence of an organization, a rule is necessary. The root word for "skills" from the Old Norse "skil," means "distinction" or "to make a difference." A skill is a learned power of doing a thing competently. Teachers of self-discipline who want to train children in civility believe the following:

- Every culture has a set of rules that people grow to understand as they mature.
- Rules are posted, so people do not have to guess expectations.
- Rules are meant to keep people safe.
- Children should *not* make the rules but should be in an environment where adults establish and enforce rules.
- Teachers invite children to help create procedures that will guide them to follow the rules.
- Procedures will change depending upon the situation, the teacher, the subject, the home life, parent expectations, and student's ability level.
- School rules should be broad and uniform in all grade levels to allow for consistent enforcement.

- A minimum number of rules works best.
- Rules should be reasonable and stated positively.
- Rules protect the rights of others. When rules no longer achieve the purpose for which they were created, they can be changed.

Wise rulemaking takes into consideration some or all the following:

- If a person wants to belong to a group, they must learn group expectations. The standard operating procedure for family or classroom must be clearly defined and understood by those who enforce and follow the rules.
- Put the rule in writing, discuss it carefully, and post it as a visible reminder.
- Periodically check to see if persons are still clear about the meaning of the rule.
- Plan to teach the rules. A written test can be given to measure how well students have learned the rules. In the home, as children grow older, they should be able to finish the sentence," In this family we believe... because..."
- Rules are revised if adults find them unreasonable.
- Adults, as positive role models, compliment community members who have followed the rules.

Students perceive and have commented that teachers 'have their act together,' when the rules are consistent between classrooms.

Three broad rules adopted by teachers are 1) Respect yourself, others, and things; 2) Contribute to the learning environment; 3) Follow school and classroom procedures.

Similar rules adopted by parents are 1) Respect family members; 2) Contribute to the household; 3) Follow family procedures.

Rules and Procedures in Kindergarten through Third Grade

Primary children in pre-school through second grade grasp the rules and procedures better in rhyme. A group of fifth and sixth graders created these rhymes for the first and second graders. To test the students, the teacher recites the first part of the rhyme and students in unison recite the second part. Rhymes used to teach the rules are as follows:

Respect Yourself, Others, Things: To show you care, you must share/ If my eyes you cannot see, don't begin to talk to me/ If you are kind, a friend you will find.

Contribute to the Learning Environment: Keep your feet under your seat/My place is my space/If you are sloppy, you will recopy/If you get a time out, please don't pout.

Follow Classroom Procedures: If you hit, you must sit/If you throw food, you will be rude/Learn to freeze for safety, please.

Rules and Procedures for Fourth through Eighth Grade

Respect Yourself, Others, and Things

- Take pride in your appearance.
- Honor others' space and things.
- Show respect by greeting others and using an appropriate tone of voice.
- Speak positively of the school, teachers, and classmates.
- Leave common spaces clean.
- Help those you notice who need help.

Contribute to the Learning Environment

- Participate in group discussions and activities.
- Contribute by communicating thoughts and ideas.
- Use agreed upon social skills.
- Complete assignments on time.
- Be attentive to teachers and peers.
- Ask for assistance and offer assistance to others.

Follow School and Classroom Procedures

- Know and follow the fire, tornado, earthquake, safe-school drills, et cetera.
- Know and be able to tell others the rules of our school.

- Conform to the dress code.
- Use a procedure to organize work.
- Use phones, tablets, and computers at appropriate times.

When Rules Are Not Followed

When a rule is broken, a consequence usually follows. A teacher will use their classroom management plan to identify consequences, moving from the least restrictive action to the more severe actions (see Chapter 17). When an infraction involves danger, serious disruption, or disrespect that prevents learning and teaching, the consequences can have legal ramifications. Students willing to take a consequence for a rule infraction indicate they want to take control of their learning.

In these cases, a consequence can be negotiable. There are three different types of consequences.

Natural Logical Consequences	Every action has a reaction. The consequence is in direct proportion to the action (e.g. When learners fail to review and study for a test, their grades may be lower than expected).
Adult-imposed Consequences:	When a child demonstrates that they are not able to fix a problem on their own, another adult will decide the best course of action. Sometimes, learners consider this punishment because the consequence is inconvenient and uncomfortable. The short-term effect of an adult-imposed consequence is to restore order and help a child gain self-control. The long-term goal is to teach self-discipline skills by providing opportunities for learners to practice the skill.
Self-Imposed Consequences:	A person can become aware they are having difficulty following procedures or rules. They can decide to change. The chosen plan of action is called a "self-imposed consequence." Learners in fourth through eighth grade learn about self-imposed consequences in *Discipline with Purpose.*

A group of sixth graders designed these self-imposed consequences:

1. Design a poster that illustrates the difference between a consequence and a punishment. When you finish, have the teacher check the quality of your product. Teach the class about the difference and then hang the poster in your classroom.
2. List five ways students disrupt learning. Explain why it takes leadership to be a responsible student. Give examples of how a student leader can exert leadership:
    *   Stand on the side of truth even if you stand alone.
    *   See the needs of others and regard these needs as important.
    *   Be prepared to inconvenience yourself for the sake of others.
3. If you offended one person, tell the person you are sorry by offering to do something for them. If you offended more than one person, show your sorrow by doing something positive for the entire group.
4. Pick the subject in which you need the most review. Design 20 questions that will help you learn. Ask the teacher for a five to ten-minute time slot to ask your review questions to the class.
5. Look at the consequence cards posted on the consequence board. Select the one that will help you learn or change your behavior. If you cannot find a card, negotiate with your teacher until you agree upon a consequence that will help you learn.

These and other suggestions were posted on a consequence board. Learners who did not follow the rules or classroom procedures, selected the consequence that would help them learn.

Once selected, a learner had three days to complete the task. If not completed on time, an adult-imposed consequence was given. Self-imposed consequences are meant to teach a lesson or skill, break a bad habit, or establish a new behavior based on the belief that the older child is the best judge of what will help his or her learning process.

The Last Word

Before any consequence is given, the teacher should consider whether the learner's behavior is caused by a lack of skill development. If a student already has limited social skills and only a few friends, reducing recess time may increase social isolation. A student's tardiness may be due to an adult's lack of organization.

The use of positive behavior interventions such as praise and rewards can often shape student behavior better than the use of a consequence. Behavior plans, which learners help design, teach them they have some power and control in changing behaviors.

Learner's Request a Rule Change

Mrs. Martin was immediately drawn to the idea of teaching the 15 self-discipline skills. However, when she started to teach her fifth graders about the skill of understanding rules, they became vocal in their objection to existing school procedures. Their major complaint was *not* having physical education class more than once a week.

At first, Mrs. Martin thought her lesson was a disaster and feared she had opened a can of worms. In discussion with her peers, she realized how to use the children's perceptions as an opportunity to allow them to practice the skill of understanding rules. After all, this was the children's issue, not hers. They could do the work of trying to figure out how to resolve the problem.

Once she changed the way she thought about the issue, her attitude and actions also changed. She informed the principal that her students would be doing some research. She encouraged the principal to be supportive because they were practicing a difficult self-discipline skill.

She told her class that, in wanting more frequent P.E. classes, they were requesting a rule change. She asked for a group of volunteers to research the issue and come up with suggestions for making changes.

The initial group of 16 participants was soon reduced to a group of five when they understood the complexity of the process for changing a rule. Mrs. Martin gave them a copy of the state requirements for the number of hours students must be in each class during a school year, as well as a copy of the P.E. teacher's schedule, and the schedule for the current classes. She asked one of the volunteers to write a letter of introduction, which she would sign. This would allow them to interview teachers and have access to some matters of public record from the school office.

The young people were eager to begin and decided they would all write the letter of introduction. During the brainstorming session, they created a plan of action. They synchronized their phone calendars and scheduled meetings. They also scheduled times when they could report their progress to the class.

Their work began in January. They set the end of February as their goal for completing this task. In the first week, enthusiasm ran high. On Friday, at the class meeting, the students presented large posters showing the current schedule for P.E. class. They reported that the principal encouraged them to do this project. The second week, they reported there were more things to take into consideration than they had first thought. Progress was slow. The third week, the students did not have a chance to meet as a group, so there was nothing to report.

In the fourth week, they were still working on the project but needed more time to complete it. Finally, in the fifth week, they told their classmates that, while their idea appeared to be a good one, there were no good alternatives. With over 700 children in the school, the current schedule was the only one that seemed feasible.

Mrs. Martin complimented the group for trying to resolve the issue. She asked them what they had learned about understanding the reasons for rules. In giving the students the responsibility to effect change, the students understood the complex process involved to alter rules.

Activities to Do at Home

- Make a list of 20 grammar rules and demonstrate how they would be used in a sentence.
- Find three rules from historical times that are now outdated. Speculate as to why the rule came into existence.
- Project into the future and draw up a list of rules that might govern life in the year 2050. Explain the conditions that would cause the rule to exist.
- Imagine what the positive, negative, and interesting outcomes might be if there was a rule that all cars had to be blue in color.
- Role play the right way and the wrong way to follow household rules.

Money Matters
By Lynn Murtagh

In our home, choosing to lose an allowance for not doing a chore is not an option. Everyone is expected to do their part.

On the other hand, my husband and I believe that our children need opportunities to learn money management. Therefore, we instituted an allowance program that is $1.00 multipled by the children's age paid each month until they are 13 years old.

This allowance is given regardless of chore performance. Out of this money, our children must buy their extra wants, like toys, CD's, etc. Essentially, they are free to spend the money as they wish. Sometimes they are very successful at saving for something special and sometimes, they blow their whole allowance in the first week or days of the month. Regularly, we have discussions about financial goal setting and saving.

CHAPTER 12

The Skill of Accomplishing Tasks Independently

 The maze pattern, or whorl, of a fingerprint is used to represent the skill of accomplishing a task independently. Its unique and singular quality symbolizes the individual mental and physical energy we each use to accomplish a task.

*When we **INDEPENDENTLY COMPLETE TASKS:***

*We **WAIT** until we have learned the parameters for finishing the task.*

*We **THINK**: What plan of action can I take to get this job done? Am I capable of completing the entire job? Will I need help from anyone else?*

*We **ACT**: We work our plan for the allotted time given.*

In the Jewish culture, the Bar Mitzvah and Bat Mitzvah ceremonies mark the rite of passage for young boys and girls. Hispanic girls participate in a Quinceañera to symbolize their journey from childhood to maturity. During the celebration, the celebrant will gift a doll to a younger friend or relative, indicating it is time to leave childhood behind. When a young girl comes of age in some Native American tribes, she signifies this passage by weaving a basket using her own unique design. These rituals signify that participants will be forever changed and that they will no longer be considered a child. A dramatic shift has occurred in the child's life.

A similar dramatic shift occurs when children acquire the skill of independent thinking and are able to complete tasks on their own. The developmental psychologist Jean Piaget described this as a move from the "concrete operational stage of reasoning" to the "formal operational" phase, a shift that begins around the age of 12 and continues to develop. The ability to use logic enables one to think about possibilities, form original ideas, consider points of view, and begin to think abstractly. Youth at this age are more capable of independent thinking and are able to make sense of things based on their own experiences and observations (Piaget, 1952).

Adults need to be ready for the developmental shift. Why? Challenging authority is developmentally predictable. In school, a student might appear disinterested, engage in behaviors that delay instruction, or relish argumentative exchanges. Children will challenge teachers' thinking with their creative insights and "what if" questions (e.g. "But what if we had a car wash and raised the money ourselves?" or "But what if his older brother was going to be home rather than parents?" or "Why can't I dye my hair pink? It will wash out.").

Four Stages in Making Independent Choices

Before the formal operational phase, children practice skill number eight by following the procedures and systems established by adults who are competent and organized. To become independent, a child must learn to make appropriate choices. Correctly choosing takes practice and is developed gradually as children grow from one stage to the next. Consider these four stages:

Stage One: Children decide between two choices preselected by adults (e.g. Would you like to read a story before your snack or after your snack?).

Stage Two: Children can be invited to suggest their own choice or to add to the one an adult offers (Would you like to finish your homework before dinner or after, or do you have another time in mind?).

Stage Three: The child makes an independent choice and lives with the consequence. Parent and child discuss the choice and its consequences to determine how effective the choice was. Modifications and new rules might be established.

Stage Four: The child sets goals, makes choices, and takes the consequences. The child self-evaluates the process.

Help Children Become Independent

Adults must resist the temptation to think, "I can get things done faster and more thoroughly if I do it myself." This may be true. When children start doing things on their own, their projects are often messy and they have their own ideas about how to accomplish tasks. A father told us the first time he asked his son to mow the front lawn, he assumed his son would complete the task much like he did, mowing in straight rows from one end of the lawn to the other.

Without pre-teaching, the boy went around the perimeter of the lawn making a box. He continued in this fashion until the rectangular shape closed in on itself in the center. He accomplished the task and, like the song, 'He did it his way!'

Avoid over-structuring a child's day. Provide a time for the activities that must occur, but let children decide on the order and time for completion. If we stop and think, we will discover many opportunities where children can practice being independent. For example, when items needed in school are left at home, parents can refuse to rush to a child's defense.

Instead, allow the child to experience the natural, logical consequence of forgetting. Then, teach strategies that will help students remember. When sibling conflicts and problems arise, the adult's role should be one of a 'resource' rather than a 'fixer.' We can check in with the child and ask how things are going; we can give children assurance that we believe they can find a resolution. We can even invite a child to ask for advice or our opinion and still honor the fact that fixing the problem is the child's.

Middle grade students are prone to focus on getting their work finished, rather than on the quality of their work. When my fifth-grade nephew offered to mow my lawn, he asked me what I would pay for the job. I told him I used a sliding scale. If he just mowed the lawn, he could earn ten dollars. But if he mowed and used the edger, it would be worth 15 dollars. If he mowed, edged, and picked up grass clippings it would be worth 20. I gave him the option of choice while helping him understand my expectations of a quality job. I wasn't concerned about the amount of time it took to complete the job. My focus was on the care and effort he put into the task.

Independent thought can be expanded by exploring the fact that one job can be accomplished in many ways. One strategy is to select a comic strip that has several frames or a picture with a humorous caption. Remove the dialogue or caption. Set a time limit of ten minutes. Work individually or in teams to create a new dialogue to go with the pictures. Share the finished products. Talk about the ideas generated. Discuss other times in school, at home, or in the community when something can have different meanings to different people. Discuss ways to handle the differences.

Learners in fifth through eighth grades need opportunities to express their opinions when discussing controversial issues. Write the words *I agree, I disagree,* and *I can't decide* on three separate posters. Hang each poster in a separate area of the room. Make a statement and ask students to stand under the words that best represents their opinions. Ask everyone to explain why they chose each position. Learners often experience an 'a-ha' moment when realizing others either share or do not share their thoughts, feelings, and opinions.

It takes courage to voice an opinion. Saying something different from another person can make one vulnerable to criticism. If our children are to be the future leaders of the country, teaching and encouraging them to be independent thinkers is essential.

Older learners gain personal insights when they discuss routine ways of completing tasks. When assigning tasks, an adult might say, "These are the givens and here is where you can practice independent thinking." Using this phrase, the adult can outline the aspects of the task everyone must accomplish and give permission to complete it individually.

Phrases to encourage the use of independent thinking include:

"This is all I can tell you. Now you must decide for yourself."
"There are many ways to do things. Who can describe one way?"
"I have a challenge for you. I understand that not everyone will be able to meet the challenge. Please raise your hand if you are willing to try."
"Have you considered this as an option?"
"Do you want to know how your performance matched my expectations?"

"What if half your friends did this and half your friends did that – what would you do?"
"Your idea is original. How can you package your finished product to make it more appealing?"

Finally, adults can coach learners to work independently by routinely asking three questions before turning power over to children to complete tasks:

1. "Are you able to do this job as well as I can or better?" This allows the adult to explain how to complete the task if the child does not know.
2. "What is your plan for getting the task done?" This allows the child to make a list of steps and think about the goal before starting.
3. "Do you want the entire job or only a portion of it?" This allows the child to recognize their capabilities and limits.

In one elementary school, where these three questions were routinely asked, the administrator invited an eighth grader to conduct the Wednesday morning all-school assembly. Accepting the task, the young man said, "Don't worry, Mrs. Kock. I'll do it just like you do." True to his words, the student did an excellent job.

Setting Realistic Goals

Success in completing tasks begins with the ability to set realistic goals. John Lee Dumas, a productivity expert, encouraged the use of the acronym SMART after determining a goal to describe components of a well-developed goal: Specific, Measurable, Attainable, Relevant, and Time Bound (Dumas 2016).

For example, a learner might have a goal to improve their ability to speak in front of the class. If the way to accomplish the goal is simply "to try harder," it would not pass the SMART test. A more effective goal would read: "I will raise my hand and ask four questions or make four comments each day for a week."

Another student might have a goal to decrease the amount of late work to improve a grade. Handing in more papers on time would not pass the SMART test. A more effective goal reads, "I will increase the number of assignments I turn in each month by 50 percent." Evaluating the goal using the SMART criteria ensures the student will know exactly what to do and in what time frame. Breaking the goal into manageable pieces outlines how the goal will be accomplished. A student can evaluate progress at the end of each week.

A Wait-and-Think Strategy

This strategy works well in classes that are departmentalized and meet for 45 minutes to an hour. At the end of each class period, invite students to think about their class experience and record a one, three, or five in their journal or assignment book. If they understood the lesson, they record a five and write one fact they learned. If the learning is fuzzy, they record a three and write one question about the day's lesson. If they feel lost, they record the name of a classmate who they will ask to help them.

Post an 8 ½ x 11 laminated sheet of paper on which the numbers one, three, and five are printed by the classroom exit door. As students leave the room, they touch the number indicating their level of satisfaction with the daily lesson. The teacher can see at a glance how much review is needed and who is having difficulty. A variation on the theme is to list the 15 self-discipline skills. Each student can be encouraged to touch the skill they practiced during the class period.

The Last Word

Learners who are not motivated, or don't know how to complete tasks independently, will often exhibit the following behaviors:

- Cannot establish and follow realistic goals
- Overwhelmed by tasks not broken into small segments
- Cannot decide when they need help or can work independently
- Inability to choose between alternatives
- Fail to evaluate their work and make revisions as needed
- Fail to voice opinions and raise questions

Use a pre-teaching checklist to itemize the steps needed to complete a task. Activities that can be pre-taught include organizing a desk or locker, conducting a family or class meeting, and reviewing expectations prior to an event. Children can test out the steps listed and make revisions or corrections.

When students require constant reassurance that they are doing work correctly, give them short periods of time to work independently. Struggling five to ten minutes to figure things out and answer questions for themselves is a healthy struggle.

Jamie Learns a Lesson

A group of junior high teachers were eating lunch at a cafeteria table. Jamie, an eighth grader, came up to the teachers' table and hovered behind her favorite English teacher. "Miss North, Miss North! I've got to talk to you," said Jamie.

"Not now," chided Miss North. "Can't you see I'm eating?"

Jamie left but returned a minute later. Again, she tried to get Miss North to notice her.

This time, Miss North sounded a little perturbed. "I'll talk with you when I am finished!"

When Jamie headed back toward Miss North for a third time, co-worker Mrs. Flynn offered to talk with her, meeting Jamie halfway. "Jamie," said Mrs. Flynn, "I noticed you really need to speak to Miss North, but this is not the right time or way to get her attention. Miss North has a right to eat her lunch in peace and right now you are disturbing that right. I want you to move away from the table and think about another way you might get her attention. Do you think you will be able to find another way?" Jamie agreed.

Later that afternoon, Miss North came to Mrs. Flynn and asked, "What did you say to Jamie?"

Suddenly concerned, Mrs. Flynn prompted, "Why?"

"Because she came up to me after lunch and asked if she could make an appointment to talk to me. We just spoke for 20 minutes and it was the best conversation we have ever had."

Mrs. Flynn told Miss North there was no secret in what she did. "I just focused on the fact that she did not know the proper way to get your attention and told her she had to figure out on her own another way to accomplish this task. I guess she did." Mrs. Flynn suggested that there might be more students who do not know the appropriate way to gain a teacher's attention. She told her to use the rule of thumb: If there are five or more students who appear to be missing a self-discipline skill, it is time to teach the skill.

I Can Manage Myself!

Name: _____

Grade: _____ Subject or Class: _____

Award yourself up to five points each day for each item listed.

Goals	M	T	W	Th	F
My assignments were complete.					
I turned in my assignments on time.					
My work was done neatly and carefully.					
I spent 10 minutes reviewing.					
I participated in class discussion.					
I was able to do independent work.					

This week, the most important thing I learned about the way I demonstrate the self-discipline skill of working independently is:

CHAPTER 13

The Skill of Exhibiting Leadership

 The "V" formation of geese migrating suggests the presence of leadership. The geese always have a solitary leader supported and relieved by the whole.

When we EXHIBIT LEADERSHIP,

We WAIT until we have noticed a situation that needs a leader.

We THINK: What course of action will make life better for people? Am I willing to act even if I am the only one? Can I inconvenience myself for the sake of another?

We ACT: We take the first step to improve the situation. We take charge.

The qualities of a leader are universal. These occur in the poor and the rich, the proud and the humble, the common person and the brilliant thinker. A leader reaches out to others and gives them direction. Feeling confident enough to speak to others about the things they see, they take charge. They organize people to respond to others' needs.

Leaders possess qualities that are not always self-evident. The DWP program teaches that true leaders exhibit three main qualities:

1. They notice the *needs* of others and consider those needs to be important.
2. They stand on the side of *truth,* even if they stand alone.
3. They *act* on behalf of another, even if they are inconvenienced.

Considering these qualities, leadership can be practiced at any age. It can be as simple as a young child cleaning up a mess without being told to do so or as complex as standing up for the victim of a bully, or counseling someone for making a poor choice. Educators who apply these three qualities have found that the 'A' student is not always the one who emerges as a leader; rather, it is the child who humbly moves among his peers as a helper.

Leaders are admired and set apart because their actions stand out. They perform ordinary tasks with extraordinary care. Our children can readily name the heroes of their day. Unfortunately, children think of icons, celebrities, and action figures as leaders, even though they may not possess leadership qualities and are negative rather than positive role-models.

Middle grade students can confuse a leader with someone who is expressive and talks a lot. They think leaders are popular and can make everyone laugh. Sometimes, middle grade students think leadership is demonstrated by the person who takes on authority and pushes the limits.

The focus of leadership is on helping and being of service to others. It is on doing what is right. It demands that we count the cost; and it may be costly, but we choose to act despite this. When the leadership skill is practiced, there will be a benefit to the leader as well as others.

Why Teach the Skill of Leadership?

When teaching the skill of Exhibiting Leadership, the teacher assists learners to take a personal stand on issues and resist group pressure. The *DWP* teacher helps learners identify unsafe, illegal, or immoral actions. Children learn to distinguish between positive and negative leadership, and are encouraged to evaluate their own leadership qualities.

One mother described a time when she deliberately switched the way she spoke to her son about his behavior. He was in the optimum age to practice the Constructive Skills, so she refrained from using Basic Skill vocabulary. Josh, her 12-year-old son, was upset because his peers wouldn't listen to him and wear helmets as they skateboarded down a winding hill. His buddies teased him and called him names. He was sullen most of the afternoon until finally telling his mother about the incident.

His mom's immediate reaction was pride. Her son had *followed the instructions* she had often given to him about skateboarding safety. Instead of complimenting him for following her instructions (a Basic Skill), she suggested he was a *leader* because he could separate fact from feeling. "You stood on the side of your truth even though you stood alone," she explained. "You didn't retort with angry words even though your friend's words were upsetting."

By using age-appropriate skill language, she recognized her son's ability to demonstrate higher level self-discipline skills and helped reframe the incident. Josh was willing to own and take pride in his actions.

Leadership Activities

At one school in Omaha, Nebraska, all the students gather in assembly to start the day. They end that morning meeting with the recitation of the following Citizenship Pledge:

I am responsible for all my actions and behavior today. I will listen, do my work, and learn. I will respect the feelings, property, and rights of others. I will be a good citizen by doing what is right, not because adults watch me, but because it is the right thing for me to do for myself and for others. I will look for opportunities to be a leader and especially lead myself in practicing positive values and skills.

Examples of leadership tasks are listed on the back of the Citizenship pledge card:

- Lead a classroom activity.
- Introduce yourself to someone new.
- Attend an after-school activity to support the school.
- Accept constructive criticism by showing appreciation for the person who critiques your work.
- Share credit with your team.
- Volunteer to help someone.
- Complete a leadership activity of your choice.

Students are encouraged to complete tasks they have not previously tried. Periodically, students are given an opportunity to report on their progress. Sixth graders were asked to describe their expectations of a school leader. They responded that leaders for their school should be able to:

- Explain the school motto, colors, mascot, and mission statement.
- Sing/recite the school song.
- List and explain the all school and classroom rules.
- Orient new students to the school in a positive manner.
- Make visitors feel welcome.
- Stand up against bullying, hazing or cliques.
- Conduct a class meeting or committee meeting.
- Set agendas and stick to them.
- Make a plan and set a goal.
- Identify tasks and delegate responsibilities.

In generating this list, the students defined the culture of their community. These same students used the acronym CLASS to describe the self-discipline skills they were practicing.

Communicates.	Cooperates.
Listens.	Listens.
Accomplishes tasks.	Asks questions.
Socializes well with others.	Selects procedures.
Serves others.	Solves problems.

The Art of Delegation

Children let adults know when they are ready to take on more responsibility. We hear them say, "Do I have to do it that way?" or "I have an idea." They may simply say they have a better idea than the one proposed. When we hear these phrases, it is time to recognize that some of our adult power can and should be shared. To delegate means to entrust or empower another to act on our behalf.

Research has shown the importance of the expectation level of adults in enhancing children's learning. "The quality of adult-youth relationships in schools is a powerful predictor of... students' satisfaction with and connection to school; academic performance;

quality of peer relationships..." (Griggs, Glover Gagnon, Huelsman, Kider-Ashley, & Ballard 2009, Konishi, Hymel, Zumbo, & Li, 2010). A few minutes of quality time spent discussing how the child plans to proceed, as well as time evaluating their level of success, is crucial to the delegation process.

The goal of delegating tasks is to train children to function in the world. When a football player throws a pass, he must have faith that his teammate will catch it. How do you get to the point where you have faith in the people to whom you are giving power?

Normally, faith and trust are earned as individuals demonstrate they are capable of accomplishing what is needed. Adults can identify the amount of delegation an individual is given to complete a task. The following Delegation Form shows four different levels of control to describe the types of leadership needed. The adult assigning the task checks the degree of delegation required.

Delegation Form

1. A description of the delegated job
2. Person delegating the job
3. Person(s) who will complete the task
4. Completion date for the task
5. Steps in the plan
6. The degree of delegation (Check one)

_____ Take full control of this job. Do the job without any further contact with me.

_____ Take action but let me know what you did and when you finish.

_____ Find a partner and brainstorm solutions to the problem. Discuss your plans with me before taking action.

_____ Think about this task. Make a list of actions I/we might take and those that should be avoided. Provide me with recommendations. I will make the final decision.

Leaders Know Themselves: A group exercise

Good leaders know their strengths and weaknesses. They know their personal qualities and gifts. The following exercise can help students own their gifts and talents and works best when a group of students has been together for an extended period and has some first-hand knowledge about one another.

Divide students into groups of six or more. Give everyone a three-by-five index card and ask them to print their names on the top of the card. One student begins the session by sharing one statement of talent, special interest, or favorite subject. That student then asks two people in the group if they agree or disagree with the statement and if they can give a reason for their agreement.

If both persons agree, the item is listed on the card. If either or both disagree, they must state how their perception differs from the student's statement. The exercise continues as action moves from person to person. When everyone has identified three personal items on which the group agrees, the exercise ends.

Social, Emotional Learning

Social, Emotional Learning (SEL), an integral part of many classrooms, encourages the development of teams where students can learn and practice essential leadership skills. These skills include self-awareness, accountability, self-motivation, and collaboration:

- Self-awareness: Leaders can control strong emotions. They understand how actions affect people. They recognize and learn how to manage stress. They can identify and express their feelings.
- Accountability: Leaders admit mistakes and accept consequences. They do not blame others when things go wrong.
- Self-motivation: Leaders have persistence. They continue moving forward until they reach their goals.
- Collaboration: Leaders compliment others and know how to resolve conflict. They can make reasonable choices that will satisfy most people.

Fifth Grade Leaders

Mrs. Augustine wanted her fifth graders to concentrate on leadership skills. At the beginning of the school year, she introduced them to the three qualities of a leader. During one of the first weeks of practice, the fifth-grade boys had completed their lunch, leaving papers and debris under and on top of the lunch table.

Rather than just ask them to pick up the mess, Mrs. Augustine said, "Please raise your hand if you are looking for opportunities to practice leadership today." Seven hands went up. Then she asked, "Who would be willing to practice leadership now and clean up the mess at the lunch table?" All the hands went down, except for one.

"I'll do it," said Jeremy. Mrs. Augustine thanked him and started up the stairs with the rest of the class. On the way to the classroom, two of Jeremy's classmates said, "Jeremy really is a leader." Mrs. Augustine asked why. "Because he was the only one willing to inconvenience himself and pick up the mess." Jeremy led by example.

Later, Mrs. Augustine told another teacher that Jeremy's example helped the boys in the class reach a new level of understanding of how leadership is practiced. In the weeks that followed, some students volunteered to clean the lunch table without being asked. Others looked for new opportunities to practice leadership.

News of the fifth graders experiment with the skill of leadership spread throughout the local schools where self-discipline skills were being taught. At the end of the school year, Mrs. Augustine's students were invited to speak to several other fifth grade classes about the skill of leadership.

"With training in civility, we develop the invaluable habit of considering that no action of ours is without consequences for others and anticipating what those consequences will be."

Choosing Civility, P.M. Forni, p. 14

Are You Helping Your Child Develop Leadership Skills?

Assign 5 points for actions you usually do and 0 points for action you never do. Rate yourself between 1 and 5.

_____ I encourage my child(ren) to have a positive attitude and to see mistakes as learning opportunities.

_____ I give my child(ren) chores and monitor how well or poorly these chores are performed.

_____ I let my child(ren) grapple with issues that are important to them and help them think through their actions rather than tell them what to do.

_____ I encourage my child(ren) to try new things and sometimes step out of their comfort zone. I show them by example that I am willing to do the same thing.

_____ I hold my child(ren) accountable for promises they make, things they say they are going to do, or things I ask them to do to build trustworthiness.

Now, add you scores. If the sum exceeds 20, that means you are helping your child(ren) develop leadership. A score of 15-19 is average. Below 15? Try to look for leadership opportunities.

CHAPTER 14

The Skill of Communicating Effectively

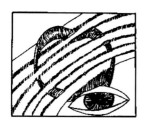 The skill of communication may be accomplished in a variety of means including writing, speech, and visual sign and/or symbols. This drawing conveys an open mouth and the universal symbol of the rainbow.

When we COMMUNICATE,

We WAIT until the other person has finished speaking.

We THINK: What words can I use that will correctly convey my thoughts and feelings?

We ACT: We say something that will connect us to the other person or group.

The power of the human voice can bring comfort where there is pain, joy where there is sorrow, instruction where there is ignorance, faith where there is doubt, healing where there is sickness, and love where there is hate. The development of our vocabulary, and the means of self-expression will be important our entire lives.

Communication is the act of sharing information or ideas. In the communication model, a sender conveys the message and a receiver interprets it. If ideas are not presented properly, if vocabulary is not precise, or if the receiver cannot relate to the message, communication can fail. The sender must have some understanding of how their words will be perceived by the receiver and be able to recognize non-verbal cues that the message is or is not getting through. Messaging between sender and receiver is not easy, because it requires individuals to have mastered the skills of listening and asking questions. Another reason is because a person's non-verbal communication often speaks louder than their words.

Teaching Communication

To develop the skill of communication, adults can engage children in deliberate conversations. I remember a conversation with a five-year-old. She listened attentively and responded by staying on the topic. At the end of our time together, I complimented her by saying, "You are a very good conversationalist." She said, "I know. Everybody tells me that."

Children in kindergarten through fourth grade learn the fundamentals of communication when adults teach the following skills:

- The skills of listening and asking questions
- Vocabulary words to build comprehension
- Waiting and thinking before speaking
- How to understand non-verbal cues
- The difference between helpful and hurtful messages
- Phrases used to close a conversation:

    "I enjoyed spending time with you."
    "Let's plan to meet again."
    "Thank you for your time."

Children in grades four through eight are taught how to use precise language, express specific needs, wants, and opinions appropriately while avoiding sarcasm, whining, gossip, and complaining. The following forms of formal and informal communication are introduced and practiced.

Verbal (Oral) Communication: The use of sounds and words to express yourself (can be quick, precise, and used to avoid misunderstandings).

Written Communication: Any type of message that makes use of the written word (newspapers, e-mails and tweets, social media, contracts, letters, thank-you notes).

Visual Communication: The conveyance of ideas and information in forms that can be seen (pamphlets, videos, illustrations, charts, power-points).

Non-verbal Interpersonal Communication: This includes facial expressions, the tone and pitch of the voice, gestures displayed through body language (kinesics) and the physical distance between the communicators (what your presence says about you in terms of posture, facial expressions, appearance, listening ability, how you make people feel when you are around).

As children mature, they will have many opportunities to spend time with people they do not know well. Their participation in clubs, sports, travel, and visits to junior high and high schools can be uncomfortable if they are not good conversationalists. Sometimes, children are unaware of expectations others have for engaging in conversation. These guidelines can be applied to conversations for both the sender and receiver:

- Show a willingness to contribute to conversation. Nodding heads or one-word answers will stifle communication.
- Let your face show interest in what the other person has to say.
- Make yourself comfortable so you are not distracted.
- Use the steps of focused listening. Look at or toward the person.
- Repeat what you think the person has said. Ask questions.
- Respect the other person's point of view. Say, "That's interesting because…" or "Have you ever thought of…?" or "It sounds like we disagree."
- Learn to express agreement or disagreement in a calm manner. You have a right to your opinion as long as you respect others' rights.
- Develop a sense of humor; don't take yourself too seriously.
- Avoid sarcasm, hostility, and defensiveness in tone or attitude.
- Try to understand the other person. Ask questions that begin with 'W' – Who, What, When, Where, Why?
- Talk about ideas, books, projects, news events, and sports. Avoid gossip.

In school, learners team up with partners and role-play conversations using these 11 suggestions. Home assignments that challenge students to conduct conversations with neighbors, relatives, or people they meet for the first time are effective ways to practice the skill of communication. Two fifth-grade teachers initiated girl-and-boy talk meetings. The meetings were held during lunchtime and the teachers, girls, or boys, could initiate the sessions. Boy or girl groups met separately. Groups discuss pertinent issues about life and growing up. Gossip was not allowed.

Children can practice communication skills during family and class meetings. A short meeting of ten to fifteen minutes with one or two items on the agenda is most productive. Rules that govern the meeting include the requirement that everyone use good listening skills. Nonverbal communication or gesturing is forbidden. To ensure everyone will have a voice, use this modified maxim attributed to Associate Supreme Court justice, Stephen Breyer. "Let no one speak twice before all who wish have spoken once."

If logistics allow, sit in a circle. Place an unlit candle, talking stick, or other tangible item in the center. Invite each person who wants to contribute to the conversation to take the candle and place it in front of them. When finished giving their ideas, the candle is returned to the center. If family or class meetings are not routine, discuss these topics during an initial meeting:

- What are you most looking forward to this week?
- What one activity do you wish was over? Why?
- What is one conversation you plan to have this week?
- What can a member of this group help you with this week?

When parents communicate with school-age children, some key phrases never become outdated. Say these phrases with confidence and in a calm but firm manner. Once spoken, there is nothing more to say, except perhaps to repeat the phrase a second or third time. Add these phrases to your vocabulary:

- "I understand."
- "Probably so."
- "I'm sorry."
- "It's okay to be mad but not mean."
- "What do you think I will say?"
- "Tell me your side of the story."
- "I don't believe you have established the tone of voice you want to use during our discussion."
- "Your idea is good; your choice of words is offensive."
- "What have you learned from our conversation?"

A Business Model for Conversing

Psychologists and business managers have developed the acronyms FORM and FORD to identify topics that foster good conversation. If we can remember FORM, we can converse with people of any age. Shy and outgoing students have found this acronym helpful. Learners practice conversations using these starter questions:

F	Family	How many persons are in your family? Where did you grow up? Tell me about your family.
O	Occupation	What is your favorite subject in school? Tell me about your part-time job. What do you hope to do in the future?
R	Recreation	What do you like to do in your spare time? Tell me about your hobbies, collections, et cetera. What kind of sports do you enjoy watching?
M/D	Motivation/Dreams	What do you most like about school, your family, this city? Tell me about the club you joined. What holiday traditions do you most enjoy? What do you dream of doing, becoming, et cetera?

Putdowns, Puns, and Sarcasm

Put-downs, puns, and sarcasm can be sophisticated forms of humor. However, the capacity to understand this type of humor frequently doesn't develop until the ninth grade or beyond. Younger students, unable to distinguish between a humorous or serious comment, will feel uncomfortable and unable to respond appropriately. Middle grade students shared reasons why putdowns as a form of communication are used. They can occur when classmates get angry, think it is a smart way to show they don't care, are insecure, want to save face, don't know how to solve a problem by talking about it, or think the put-down gives them power.

One teacher taught the students these facts about put-downs:

- People put others down because they do *not* feel comfortable with themselves. They lack self-confidence.
- Sometimes, people are uncomfortable with feelings and do not know how to express them.
- Even if people laugh at put-downs, they may be unhappy or respond in kind.
- Put-downs cause others to think less of you. Kids who are well-liked make others feel comfortable.

After reflecting on put-downs as a form of communication, the fifth graders created posters that declared their school and classroom a NO PUT-DOWN ZONE.

Confrontation

When people share and express their ideas and opinions, confrontation is inevitable. Before 1963, confrontation meant "bringing two opposing parties face-to-face," from the Latin word 'confrontationem.' Today, confrontation refers to a hostile or argumentative meeting or situation between opposing parties. *DWP* educators refer to confrontation as 'facing someone who has to be faced.' A person's attitude and intention will make the confrontation either negative or positive.

Before speaking, persons can *wait* and *think*: Is there a missing skill that can be taught? What is the skill? Do I have time now to teach the skill? If not, when? We can remind ourselves that the reason for the confrontation is to teach an alternative way of action, not to retaliate or punish. Make a list of the issues or topics for discussion and refrain from having a confrontation if feelings are too strong and not under control. To stay calm, take deep breaths or focus on something else for a moment. If possible, make appointments to speak in private rather than confront in public.

Describe what you see/hear without passing judgment.	"I notice when you use a loud voice and shout..."
Give reasons for your requests and *don't argue.*	"It disturbs others in the class and they get distracted."
Use language skills to keep the conversation neutral.	"We are practicing sharing space and cooperation."
Be brief in describing the behavior that must be changed.	"I can't allow you to shout."
Ask questions to get the other person's point of view.	"Can you think of some way you can avoid this?"

It is never productive to automatically accept your point of view as the total picture. Remember the story of the blind men and the elephant? Each blind man felt only one part of the elephant and believed they had found something quite different from the others. None of their descriptions could accurately describe what was in front of them.

Showing Sorrow

Adults often coach children to use the words "I'm sorry." Children however, can repeat "I'm sorry" more than once, trying to convince an adult of their sincerity. When children are asked, "What will you do to *show* your sorrow?" they are often hard-pressed to come up with an action step.

We suggest simple tasks, such as spending five to ten minutes with the other person doing something fun. The action step can be one that may be an infringement on the child's time or one they may find uncomfortable, such as offering to do another child's chore. Writing a note or drawing a picture for the offended person can help set the stage for authentic forgiveness in later years.

> "Apologies should be thoughtfully conceived, clearly stated, and heartfelt. They need not be long and elaborate but should convey that we know exactly what we did that was wrong, that we understand the effects of our actions, and that we are not looking for excuses."
>
> Choosing Civility, P.M. Forni, p. 106

A Father and Son's Story

The Franklins are a wonderful family with six children. When the oldest son was 17, he was arrested for having an open bottle of liquor in his car. It was after midnight when the police called the boy's parents and asked for someone to come to the station to pick him up. The parents were shocked, especially Mr. Franklin who was angry and hurt. As he dressed to go to the police station, his wife reminded him, "Tony, our son will be scared. Nothing like this has happened before. Listen to him."

These words must have rumbled around inside Mr. Franklin's head all the way to the police station. When he got there, he found his son embarrassed. The boy hung his head and stood against the wall waiting for his Dad to speak. Everything the father had planned to say left him. In his total vulnerability, he communicated the only way he could. He hugged his boy and they both cried.

Reflecting on the incident, Mr. Franklin said on the journey home he felt like a new relationship was formed with his son. As his son explained his side of the story, the father listened and the two spoke honestly about what had happened. He wondered about other times he could have spoken to his son about unconditional love. The day of the court case arrived. Tony's mother and father stood on either side of their boy. The judge looked at the family and said, "Son, you have wonderful parents. They must love you very much to be here for you." With those words, he issued the sentence of one month's community service.

CHAPTER 15

The Generative Skills

THE GENERATIVE SKILLS
Coached: Grades 3-9
Optimum time to teach: Grades 6 to 9 and beyond

11. Organizing: Time, Space, People, Things
12. Resolving Problems
13. Initiating Solutions
14. Distinguishing Fact from Feeling
15. Sacrificing, or Serving Others

Civil discourse requires some knowledge of the five self-discipline skills known as the Generative Skills. Something generative can produce or develop something else. "Learners who acquire the last five self-discipline skills can act on their own responsibility in emergent situations. Since how they act is based on a consideration of the values of society and the consequences of the act for themselves and others, they are socially responsible" (Tanner, 1978, p. 38). Individuals have the power to decide to use these skills to help create a civil society, develop their unique personalities, and fulfill their dreams. People who acquire these skills are able to make changes in institutional and democratic environments throughout life, regardless of their employment.

Why the Generative Are Difficult to Master

Mastery means one has proficiency in performing a task and chooses to practice it when no one reminds or coaches them. During this period, pre-adolescents and adolescents learn how to behave in ways that will establish them as adults. Adolescents confront many tasks, including but not limited to:

- Separating emotionally from parents or guardians without rejecting them.
- Establishing a value system that can serve as a means of making moral decisions. Some people call this "finding a conscience."

- Choosing a vocation or direction and identifying one's talents, skills, and abilities.
- Understanding and accepting the joys and responsibilities of a sexual nature.

Passing from adolescence to adulthood is a process which varies in difficulty from child to child. Parents can talk about these goals and give their children permission to move away emotionally as children develop their own thoughts, dreams, and expectations.

Concepts Taught

When the Generative Skills are taught at the primary level, students learn to:

- Organize their desks, the coat rack, and their backpacks.
- Set up a homework spot with all the necessary supplies.
- Use a peace formula for resolving problems.
- Make a plan of action to meet their goals.
- Use a consequence card to self-direct their behavior.
- Let Others know when words are offensive or hurt their feelings.
- Resist a "me-first" attitude by letting others go first in line, offering to review with persons who missed classwork, acknowledge individuals who have helped them by sensing Unsung Hero certificates.
- Challenge themselves to do random acts of kindness.

Older students learn to:

- Organize their thoughts, feelings, and opinions.
- Make timelines and organize events from history.
- Resolve problems thrust upon them or of their own making.
- Employ group problem solving strategies and use Parliamentary Procedure.
- Draw up behavior contracts.
- Take the first steps to initiate solutions.
- Organize events on behalf of the entire school or other institution.
- Differentiate between facts, feelings, and opinions.
- Understand various reactions people have to mixed emotions.

- Move out of their comfort zone and consider other's needs before theirs.
- Responsibly volunteer and follow through their commitments.

The focus of the Generative Skills is to help students take responsibility for their actions, accept disappointing situations and outcomes, as well as celebrate their successes.

The Role of the Adult

When teaching the Generative Skills, the adult functions as a negotiator, mediator, and clarifier. Adults willing to negotiate with middle grade students keep the lines of communication open. They maintain veto power if actions or solutions will cause danger, disrupt the class, or disrespect others. Using this veto power wisely helps to define limits for the middle schooler even if they respond negatively. In heated discussions, adults can talk about skills needed and missing. Using skill language avoids blaming or accusing. Here are some common expressions that can neutralize heated discussions:

- "Let's explore the alternatives."
- "Put yourself in my place."
- "Can we live with the things we cannot change?"
- "Can you help me so I can understand your reasons?"
- "Is there a solution we haven't thought of yet?"
- "Should we ask others for their ideas?"

Adults can use a language and vocabulary that children can *grow* to understand. Words such as interdependence, reciprocity, mutuality, and recompense can be explained in simple language:

Interdependence	The quality or condition of being mutually reliant on each other.
Reciprocity	Behavior in which two people or groups of people give each other help and advantages.
Mutuality	A positive interactive relationship between people.
Recompense	To repay, reward.

According to Tanner, "When children are learning the Generative skills, the outlook of the teacher and parent is of great importance. Children can learn social optimism or social pessimism from their teachers. A good role model should value generosity and uphold the concept of justice in school and in the community. Being optimistic allows adults to place emphasis on the positive (what to do and how to do it) rather than on the negative (what not to do, what cannot be changed, what cannot be accomplished)" (p. 38-39).

Motivating Students to Practice the Generative Skills

Pre-adolescents and adolescents are intrigued by the association of the word 'power' with the self-discipline skills. The Greek derivation for power means the ability and the capacity to do something. This implies a person knows each skill well enough that they can choose to use it when necessary. Middle grade and junior high students understand how difficult it is to use a self-discipline skill when peers choose not to. There is a difference between the rightful use of power derived from using good communication skills and the misuse of power by manipulating others.

Students are introduced to the acronym I.C., which stands for "impulse control." The outcome of not using the *Wait, Think, Act* process is explored. One way to begin discussion is to search newspapers and periodicals for personal stories that illustrate impulsive or thoughtless actions. Students reflect on their use of these patterns in their daily lives. Older students are receptive to practicing the Generative Skills when they can self-evaluate skill strengths and weaknesses and set personal goals for improvement. Empowerment and internal motivation develop when students engage in experiments that require reflection:

1. Experiment with the skill of independently accomplishing tasks:

Work to root out a bad habit in 17 days. Identify the habit you want to extinguish. Identify the self-imposed consequence for failing to accomplish your daily goal. After five days, if you find you are not making progress and need an external motivator, identify a good friend or adult to help you. What consequence would the friend or adult suggest you use? Keep track of your progress and chart your growth. Write about the ease or difficulty you had in changing a negative behavior to one that is productive.

2. Experiment with the skill of organizing time:

For one week, monitor the amount of time you spend with family, friends, or alone. Complete a graph or pie chart displaying this information. Compare your results with two other classmates who chose this experiment. Write about what you learned about organizing your time.

3. Experiment with the skill of serving others:

Select your favorite skill from the list of 15. Develop a lesson plan you can teach to students in a lower grade to help them learn about the skill. Include in your lesson a story, some facts about the skill, and a way to practice the skill. Teach the lesson and write your observations.

Students in grades six through eight are enlightened when provided an explanation of the placement and connection of the 15 skills. After explaining how the skills are related, students immediately start to analyze the skills they perform well and those not yet mastered.

Katy, a sophomore wrote how knowing and using the self-discipline skills had influenced her life.

"Cheerleading is a big part of my life. I have worked very hard to achieve my best. I made new friends using my *social skills* and have become a better person all around using my *leadership* and *communication* skills. You must be able to communicate with the other people on the squad so you can do the best for your school. If there happens to be a disagreement with the other cheerleaders, it is important to consider *the facts from the feelings.* If a squad member creates a new cheer and you do not think it would work in the situation, you need to *make the first move to resolve the issue.*"

> Self = The unique person that is YOU.
> Discipline = A body of knowledge.
> Self-Discipline = The body of knowledge you have about your abilities to perform 15 specific skills.

Sample Self-Assessment

Below is a list of self-disciplined actions. Read each item and use one of the following letters to indicate how you feel about the action. Discuss your rating with another person.

E = This is easy for me to do
D = This is difficult for me to do
S = Sometimes this is easy and sometimes it is difficult
N = I have never done this before.

1. ____Sit quietly for 10 minutes and listen to a speaker.
2. ____Listen to a speaker when you are not interested in the topic.
3. ____Read and then follow written directions.
4. ____Ask someone a question when you don't know the answer.
5. ____Share my friends with someone new.
6. ____Introduce yourself to someone you do not know well.
7. ____Work with 3 other persons to finish a task.
8. ____Support both teams at a game by recognizing the talent of the rival team.
9. ____Follow school rules because you understand the reasons behind them.
10. ____Coach a person who chooses to break a rule and help them gain understanding of why the rule is in place.
11. ____Figure out on my own how to accomplish a task.
12. ____Offer to help another person when you notice they need help.
13. ____ Carry on a conversation with someone you do not know well.
14. ____Plan a week long work schedule for getting tasks finished.
15. ____Go to school or work and stay focused even though you had a fight with your best friend the night before.
16. ____Take the first step to resolve a problem with your friend.
17. ____Offer to help someone with household chores without being asked.
18. ____Design a plan to raise money for a worthy cause.

CHAPTER 16

The Skill of Organizing: Time, Space, People, Things

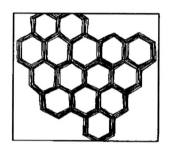

Bees have one of the most efficient means of organization. This drawing considers the beehive where form follows function and much activity occurs. Order and organization promote action and creation. The drawing symbolizes the organization of time, space, people, and things.

When we practice the skill of ORGANIZING,

We WAIT until we get a mental image of the way things are to be ordered.

We THINK: What design, timeframe, space will work best? Who should be involved in this activity?

We ACT: We plan and identify the steps that need to be taken.

Carla, mother to ten-year old Jerry, felt like she was constantly nagging him to clean up his room. "He never seems to see what I see when I look in his room," Carla told her friend Lynn. "I find myself getting angry because he doesn't listen and follow my instructions."

Lynn suggested that the messy room may have less to do with her son's lack of following instructions and more to do with the fact that the task required him to demonstrate a higher-level skill of organizing space.

"When I had the same concern, I decided to involve my son in the solution," she told Carla. "I asked him, 'What makes it difficult for you to keep your room orderly?' Then I heard, 'Mom, I don't have enough drawer space for little things, and some of the stuff in my room I no longer use.' My son was a collector. Most of what he collected ended up under the bed or all over his dresser. But he didn't want things to be hidden away. He wanted to be able to see them at a glance. So, small plastic open baskets became our storage system. He labeled the baskets and ordered them so he could find things. We agreed that every time we purchased new clothing, something had to be donated. Once a system was in place, he was able to follow instructions for cleaning up the room."

Carla began to think about other instructions she had expected her son to follow, which might have been too challenging because they required a different self-discipline skill.

The Optimum Time to Teach

Adolescents' gifts to the world are spontaneity and a sense of adventure. The pre-teen and early adolescent may spend inordinate amounts of time in front of the mirror, lamenting whatever is out of proportion and admiring favorite features. *Organizing* time, space, things, friendships, and thoughts are difficult skills.

Many appear to choose disorganization. They think in terms of short-range goals, not recognizing the importance of short-term steps to attain long-term goals. Juggling the demands of family, teachers, personal friendships, and work is a difficult task.

Parents and teachers expect young people to divide the 24-hour day into the right amounts of study, work, play, socialization, and reflection. This challenge will not diminish with age. Adults struggle as well, when juggling work, friendships, family, community, and social activities.

The skill of organization helps students set realistic deadlines, organize lockers, folders, and thoughts. The skill also encourages learners to value routines, time schedules, and strategies when organizing groups or gatherings.

Three Methods Used to Organize

When we organize, we can do so using one of three methods:

A **Linear** method – Organize things in a sequential fashion. Plan an agenda and follow it. There is a place for everything and everything has a place. Use files to keep order. Routine bedtime hours and eating schedules teach children that actions happen at a certain time and in a certain place.

A **Circular** method – Some events occur with regularity like birthdays, holiday celebrations, the flow of the seasons, and moon cycles. Established checklists help to ensure traditional actions will be repeated. Children can look forward to the celebration of special times.

A **Random or Haphazard** method – Sometimes things are ordered, but only the person who determined the order can locate items quickly. Routines can change to accommodate unplanned, spontaneous events.

People can organize space and things according to their preferences. When alone, a random or haphazard method might be used. When other people are involved, a more orderly system might be implemented. Small spaces tend to get messy and clutter more readily than large areas. The following pitfalls can erode good organization:

- **Procrastination:** Wait until later to do something you could do now. Remediate this by asking a friend to encourage you to stick to your time schedule, rewarding yourself or taking a break when you finish a task.
- **Escaping:** Daydream or do something else you feel more like doing. Avoid this by doing what you say you will do, learning how to multi-task, and if needed, hire a professional organizer.
- **Deceiving yourself and others:** Fail to check the time or the amount of work that needs to be done, then you can always say, "I ran out of time." Instead, set a time limit and finish in that amount of time or race the clock and try to beat your time record.

Organizing Time

Cultures value aspects of time differently. Native Americans regard time as a continuum, having no real beginning or end. They are not clock-watchers; the present is much more significant than the future. In some cultures, on-time means waiting one-minute or less, while other cultures allow a leeway of 15 minutes.

We can begin to train children to organize time from fourth grade onward, but they will probably not master this skill until much later. Time management will happen when children have the tools to understand how to organize.

When organizing time, some people work in spurts, using periods of high energy and concentration to get things done. Some people feel comfortable only if they finish tasks well ahead of a deadline. Others need the deadline to motivate them to get a job done. Timed activities can cause some people stress, while others enjoy the challenge.

A disorganized child may appear to be unmotivated. A block of time that is not highly structured can be overwhelming for the child. Knowing how each person responds to the need to organize will allow adjustments and modifications. Routines and time schedules can be comforting to a child with cognitive impairments. Realistic goals can be set. When teachers ask students to work for just one minute, students are often surprised by what they can accomplish.

Here are some instructions to help students practice the skill of organization:

- Check to see if children can tell time without relying on digital instruments.
- Develop agendas for family and class meetings.
- Place a time frame on each item on the agenda so children can see how the meeting will be broken into topics.
- Draft a time schedule for homework and post a calendar with the schedule of different family members indicated by different colors.
- Plan a special event ahead of time.
- Anticipate and assign jobs long before the event will take place. Teach students to make to-do lists.
- At the end of the day, discuss how students accomplished tasks.

Organizing Space

The need to organize space occurs daily. Every time we look for the right size container to store leftover food, we are making a judgment that requires us to organize space. When we parallel park or maneuver between cars, our space perception must be accurate. Imagine coordinating a school of 500 children from one location to another, which needs detailed attention to movement and shared space.

Primary children draw desk maps to show how to store school items neatly in a confined space. They use maps other children have drawn to follow instructions, and return desk items to their proper locations. Older students organize lockers, notebooks, and backpacks. Students develop a place/space at home with supplies for homework. We also discuss how we care for our environment by recycling and protecting natural resources.

When Mr. Clark wanted to demonstrate how to conserve space, he placed a medium size box with a lid on the floor. He invited students to randomly toss one of their shoes into the box. This continued until the box was full and the lid closed. Students took turns guessing how many shoes were in the box.

Mr. Clark dumped out the shoes and invited the person with the most accurate guess, to put the shoes back in the box, lining them up neatly. When space remained, students continued to add more shoes. They counted the extra shoes that fit in the box and learned about the efficiency of orderly versus random use of space. Students discussed areas of the school and places at home they might organize efficiently.

Organizing People and Ideas

Children practice organizing people when they select members for their teams and organize them into groups. They learn about parliamentary procedure and other methods used to conduct orderly meetings. They utilize different voting methods to determine group consensus. They form study groups or student partners to help in the learning process.

Whenever students engage in review exercises, they are organizing information they previously learned. The tic-tac-toe game described below is a review game that includes the need to organize time, space, people, and things:

- Organize time: Five-ten minutes
- Organize people: Divide into two teams. One team will be the X's and the other are O's.
- Organize materials: Design 30 review questions from material previously studied.
- Organize space: Place nine chairs in the front of the room in three rows of three.

Start by asking the first person on Team One a question. If the answer is correct, they will strategically take a seat in one of the nine chairs. Students cross their arms to indicate they are an 'X' and make a circle to represent the 'O.'

Continue by asking the first person on Team Two a question. The game continues in this manner until one team completes a tic-tac-toe with its members.

Children can learn much by watching teachers as they model the skill of organization. Teachers model the skill of organization in the following ways:

- Start and end class on time.
- Invite a student to be the clock-watcher if a teacher tends to speak for more than a minute per age of their group.
- Allow time for students to collect their thoughts and materials before moving to another class.
- Hand back all corrected papers within 48 hours of completion.
- Organize lessons to have a beginning, middle, and end.
- Make appointments to meet with students at odd times: 7:37 or 3:12. This helps students to be more conscious of the time.

Organizing Things

When children receive new clothes or toys, parents will invite the child to donate an older item to charity. Adults can refuse to buy into the "everyone must have their own things" mentality. We teach children to care for their belongings and, sometimes, to do their own laundry. They can organize clothing by color, select the right amount of detergent, dry and return clothing to closets or drawers.

Older children can learn to barter by offering to work for what they want, make something for someone, or trade personal items. In school, we often organize ideas and information on flash cards, in portfolios and journals. Furthermore, the skill of organization helps students organize their thoughts so they can speak and write coherently. Organizing thoughts for speaking and writing requires students to *wait* and *think.*

An Organized Approach for Adults

When adults interact with children, there are three different styles or approaches they can use. Called "Windows," the title suggests that communication is two-way. By our words, gestures, and actions, we communicate the amount of control we are willing to keep and the amount we are willing to assign to others.

We can think of the first window as the 'I' window. An 'I' teacher/parent believes a child becomes self-disciplined when the environment is structured, so children learn expected behaviors. Using this style, a teacher/parent/adult organizes planned activities to pre-teach children expectations so activities will be successful. Adults anticipate and address problems before they arise. Children often perceive an adult using the 'I' window as having most of the power and are encouraged to follow that person's lead. A disciplinarian who prefers this style will utilize detention systems, points, time-outs, positive and negative reinforcement, physical intervention, and isolation. A person in the 'I' window might start a conversation with these phrases:

I would like to challenge you to...
I need you to...
I don't know why either, but we are asked to...
I feel anxious about the noise in the room...
I think we have a problem here...

When adults use the 'We' window, they collaborate and negotiate with children. They recognize how the rights and responsibilities of both adult and child are intertwined. Adults always keep veto power if a suggested activity is unsafe, illegal, or disruptive. Children often perceive a person using this style as sharing power.

A disciplinarian using the 'We' style will restrict privileges, draw up social contacts, hold class meetings to discuss issues of concern, and expect students to make restitutions. Adults who prefer the 'We' style believe self-discipline is nurtured when individuals are in relationships. Conflicts are inevitable but can be resolved through negotiation and communication. A person in the 'We' window might start a conversation with these phrases:

> What can we do to bring out your potential?
> Is this a plan we can all take ownership of?
> We can work this out without shouting.
> We don't need to solve this now. It can wait.
> We can't fix this by making a problem for someone else.

When an adult uses the 'You' window, they delegate power and let children take the lead. Strong-willed children often respond best when an adult gives them power to make their own decisions. A disciplinarian using the 'You' style will prefer to use humor, natural/logical consequences, and non-verbal communication to encourage a student to self-monitor and draw up a behavior improvement plan. The 'You' teacher recognizes and strives to meet a child's innate needs.

Many children learn best to become self-disciplined, when adults act as a resource, coach, or counselor. A person in the 'You' window might start a conversation with these phrases:

> Does this sound like something you can do?
> Tell me your side of the story.
> How can you help yourself?
> What are your options?

All the windows have value. Optimum times to use the 'I' approach includes times when:

- Students are around dangerous equipment or in potentially dangerous situations.
- You are in a situation where someone is being disruptive or disrespectful.
- You are in charge of moving large groups of individuals.
- Your judgment is clear, and you can be counted on to act rationally in times of stress.
- You are interacting with a person unable to make safe, legal or moral decisions.

The 'We' approach works well when:
- Trying to build a democratic environment with a group.
- Teaching students to work in cooperative learning groups.
- Involved in team efforts with other teachers, parents or business leaders.
- Solutions are needed for problems that involve the students.
- Developing rubrics to evaluate student work.

The "You' approach works well when:
- There has been a crisis in the community and feelings are raw.
- Working with strong-willed individuals who need some measure of control.
- Students are invited to express their opinions without fear of being judged.
- A tense situation can be calmed through the use of humor.
- Delegating power to complete a task to another.

There is comfort in knowing there are only three windows. If our first approach is unsuccessful, we can switch to another window. We can adjust the strategy to the style of the learner when we know whether the child likes to accomplish tasks on their own, prefers to work with others, or prefers to take direction from a leader. Adults can monitor their approach, especially when there is conflict, when the task is new, or when the adult has strong feelings about an issue. These are the times when we resort to our personal preferences. If adults do not consider the needs of the students with whom they are working, conflicts can escalate and result in miscommunication.

How Mom Organized Swim Days

The summer had just started. Liz knew her two children would be spending many hours in the neighborhood swimming pool. The children were excited the first day they went swimming. They talked all the way home about their day. It was obvious they had enjoyed the pool.

As they entered their house, the children dumped their wet towels in the front entryway. Bathing suits landed on the kitchen table. They dropped sandals and toys in various spots, from the kitchen up the stairs and to the bedrooms. Liz took one look and made a quick decision. She brought the children down to the kitchen table and gave the older girl a pencil and paper. She told her young son to listen and help with ideas. "I need you to make a reminder card for you and your brother so you will know what to do when we get home from swimming. There are six things I want you to remember."

1. "When you come home, go immediately to the bathroom."
2. "Put wet towels on the hooks behind the bathroom door."
3. "Rinse off your suits and yourself in the shower."
4. "Put the wet suit over the shower rod or on top of the washer."
5. "Put all toys and swimming things in the plastic basket in the laundry room so they are ready for our next trip."
6. "All sandals and shoes will go on the small rug in the laundry room."

Liz waited as her daughter drew pictures and wrote key words next to each item. After recording all items, Liz asked her son to use the card and repeat how they would organize their swimming days. Her son knew all six without any help. In fact, when he needed time to think, and his sister wanted to coach him, he said, "I know, I know. Don't tell me." The children asked questions to clarify items and give their opinions of the steps. Teaching them to organize space and things took about 15 minutes. "It was the best 15 minutes I spent that summer," Liz admitted.

"We can expect self-disciplined behavior from children to the degree that they have come to think of themselves as self-disciplined."

Barbara Vasiloff, M.A.

CHAPTER 17

The Skill of Resolving Problems

 The yin and yang symbol from Daoist philosophy illustrates the skill of problem solving. Everything in the universe – the outer circle – embodies both the yin (the white) and the yang (the black). Nothing in the universe is all of one or the other. In the same way, we recognize individual opinions and differences to resolve problems.

When we RESOLVE PROBLEMS OF MUTUAL CONCERN,

We WAIT until we can understand the problem from more than one point of view.

We THINK: How can I state the problem from two different perspectives? What solution will make us both winners?

We ACT: We find a private place to begin the conversation.

Six-year-old Christopher was getting his haircut at a salon his mom and dad frequented. Chris, normally very polite to his barber Joe, had an "off day." He swirled and squirmed in his chair, and replied to Joe's questions in short, snappy quips. His mother and Joe quickly noticed his behavior. Joe rolled his eyes and raised an eyebrow.

This unsettling visit challenged Chris's mom to think of ways to reach her son at his level. When they got home, Christopher went to his room and crawled into his tent to play and read. His mom followed him up the stairs and got into the tent with him. "I'm wondering why your behavior was different today when we were at Joe's. I think Joe was surprised that you acted rudely," she said.

"I'm sorry" said Christopher.

His mom replied, "I appreciate you saying that, but I think it is Joe who needs the apology. What can you do for him?"

Suddenly eager, Chris chirped, "We can send him balloons. We can make cookies."

The mother explained, "Yes, but I would be doing the work. What can *you* do?"

With a nod, Chris said, "I can write him a letter." And he did.

Dear Joe,

> I'm sorry for intrupting (sic) and being unpolite (sic) to you. Next time I'll be more polite by waiting until you are done talking so I can talk, and I won't circel (sic) around in the chairs. I won't do it again.

> Chris

The next time his mom visited the salon, Christopher's letter was proudly displayed on Joe's mirror. Joe told her that the head of the salon had wanted to make a "no children allowed" policy. After reading Chris's letter, she changed her mind.

Engaging in mutual problem solving is a high-level Generative Skill. Mutual can mean "having the same feelings for one another." When people problem solve, mutually, both parties must be willing to ask themselves one question: What does this situation require of me so that this issue can be resolved? Closed hands, minds, and hearts must be replaced by open ones.

Time-Outs

The foundation for the Generative Skill to resolve problems begins when children are young. Parents use time-outs as a productive way to help children resolve problems. Whether the time-out is a stair step or one's bedroom, children in time-out must *wait* and *think* about the problem. They can write or draw their sides of the story. They can think about ways to make things better and reflect on their actions. It is important for an adult to debrief with a child after using a time-out.

I once asked a third grader how he felt about time-outs. He said, "I don't mind because my mom never comes back to find out what I thought."

Here are some questions to ask after time-out:

> "What caused you to be sent to a time-out?"
> "What is your side of the story?"
> "What do you think should happen next?"
> "Do you need me to tell you how to fix this or can you decide how to make things right?"

For children, it is not always obvious why their actions prompt a swift response from an adult. The debriefing process helps the child to learn how to be responsible for their actions. Additionally, it gives children time to think about how their actions affect others.

Techniques Used to Resolve Problems

Simple techniques used with young children to resolve problems include flipping a coin and Rock-Paper-Scissors or whatever the latest fad school children are using. For older children, the problems are more complex.

Consider the developmental stage of the pre-teen and adolescent. The adolescent brain may not fully mature until the age of 25 and beyond. Adolescents have vivid imaginations; their stress level is often high and their self-esteem unbalanced. Friends become more important than adults.

During times of trouble, teens supporting one another can arrive at solutions to problems that cause more problems for others. I'm reminded of a youth who had difficulty at home. His friend invited him to stay overnight at his house without ever considering letting the troubled teen's parent know he was safe.

We teach older students to use negotiation, mediation, and arbitration. Negotiation is a process that two sides use to reach an agreement over a dispute. When two parties cannot work toward a solution, they are encouraged to include the help of others in the negotiation. They are taught to use a mediator or third party who is present during discussions to offer suggestions. In the case of arbitration, the issue can go to a neutral third party who will hear the evidence and make the final decision.

When older students resolve problems, they learn to:

- Recognize when a problem exists and attempt to identify the cause.
- Explore all the facts.
- Brainstorm ways to solve the conflict.
- Use "what if" thinking to explore the consequences.
- Discard unrealistic solutions or any solution that will cause a problem for someone else.
- Choose a solution, follow through, and evaluate the results.

Contracting

A contract is an agreement that specifies mutual obligations. Persons meeting to complete a contract should be in a positive frame of mind and motivated to work toward a solution. A facilitator keeps the discussion moving and ensures that all people have spoken at least once before others speak twice. The facilitator puts the agreements in writing, determines if statements are introduced for majority vote, or if the parties need more time to think before a vote.

A contract includes a statement of purpose and a list of actions each person agrees to fulfill. All parties sign the completed contract and establish a renewal date to review the stipulations. A sample family contract might look like this:

FAMILY MEMBER AGREEMENT

GOAL: To get weekday mornings organized and running cooperatively.

1. Clothes for the day will be laid out the night before. The evening before each person will place their shoes by the door.

2. Everyone will be responsible for getting his/her own breakfast of cereal, toast, or toaster items.

3. After breakfast, each person will rinse and place dirty dishes in the sink or dishwasher.

4. We will leave the house at 7:30 a.m. exactly. Finish dressing in the car if not ready.

Date: _____
Renewal Date: In two weeks
Signatures: _____

Consequence Cards

Students in grades one to three can learn how to use a consequence card. The card lists four or five optional actions a student can take to show they are willing to change unproductive behaviors. The card might read: If I disrupt the learning class, I will:

Write an apology.
Miss a privilege.
Miss ___ minutes of free time.
Perform an act to show I am sorry.

A student moves through a sequence of steps when directed to do so by the teacher:

- Select a consequence from the card.
- Draw a picture or write a letter to a parent or the principal describing the infraction and how you plan to fix it.
- Leave the letter on the corner of your desk while you practice the new behavior.
- If you are unable to correct the behavior, you will be asked to discuss the letter with a parent, the principal or other adult. Their signature on the letter will indicate you have found a solution to your problem.

Wait, Think, Plan Card

Specialists or adults who work with learners only one day a week have found the use of a *Wait, Think, Plan* card to be a simple, effective method that works with students of all ages. The words Wait, Think, and Plan are printed on the front of a small card.

The back of the card contains three or four questions like: What caused you to receive this card? Which self-discipline skill would help you avoid this activity? What would it look/sound like if you used the skill? What is your plan for rejoining the class?

Cards are laminated and reused as needed. Learners are told that because time is limited, the teacher will keep the class on task by using the card. If behavior disrupts learning, the teacher will give a verbal reminder or cue to assist a student to self-correct. If this cue is not effective, the teacher will place a Wait, Think, Plan card on the student's desk or hand one to them. This is their signal to sit and think about the questions on the back of the card.

The teacher later confers with the student to find out their plan for rejoining the class. If the disruption occurs a second time, the teacher documents the incident, the student writes the answers to the questions, and the paper is sent home to be signed by a parent.

Discipline Plan

When educators develop discipline plans, they teach students the procedures to be followed when a student disrupts classroom learning. The plan is logical, reasonable, and includes a teaching component to help students address missing self-discipline skills. Teachers review the plans to let students know they will be treated fairly and with respect, when rules are not followed or misbehavior occurs. They also learn that there is a bottom line for what adults will tolerate.

In the five-step plan described below, the plan moves from least to most restrictive responses:

Step 1 – A chance to self-correct: Teacher will coach the student to take a moment to *stop, think,* and self-correct.

Step 2 – Face-to-face confrontation: The student will be reminded of the rule, procedure, and consequence.

Step 3 – Document: The student will record, write about, or draw the difficulty. Students sign a logbook indicating an appointment with the teacher is forthcoming. This step can include parent contact.

Step 4 – Involve others: Contact with parent/counselor/student assistance team (SAT). When at least three different approaches (I, YOU, WE described in Chapter 16) have been used by the teacher to effect behavioral change and there is no forthcoming change, a referral is made to another professional.

Step 5 – Removal from room: The principal or disciplinarian reviews the all-school discipline cycle, mandates in or out-of-school suspension, and meets with parents to develop an action plan.

Students may skip to step five if their behavior is deemed dangerous, seriously disruptive, or illegal.

When Children Argue

Many years ago, an educational consultant advised that when children in grades three to five argue, adults might ask them to sit in chairs back-to-back. When they give one another permission to get up, they can leave the sitting positions. In the heat of an argument, children are reluctant to make the first move and may sit silently or repeat, "I'm never giving you permission to get up!" While sitting there, children must use the *Wait, Think, Plan* pattern during which time they will cool down and focus. Inevitably the children will forget what the argument was about, begin talking, or plan what they'll do when they leave those chairs.

When coaching two or more children who are arguing or in need of discipline, the adult can structure a discussion so children can practice the listening skill. Invite one child to tell his or her side of the story and ask the other to listen. Ask the listener to tell in their own words what they heard the other person say. Check with the speaker to make sure the statement is accurate. Let the second person tell their story while the other listens. Again, ask the listener to repeat what they heard. Check for accuracy. Then ask, "What can we do to solve this problem?"

Adults teach young children about problem solving by suggesting alternative actions. When Tonya was playing with her friend and they both wanted to play with the same items, Tonya's mother addressed both girls, saying, "If you fight over your things you may not be able to play together. Would you like me to keep time so each of you can play with the item for five minutes and then switch?" She could also have said: "If I had your problem, I would put out all the doll's clothing and let each person take turns selecting an item until they were all gone. You can use my suggestion or come up with one of your own."

More Tips for Confrontation

The adult confronting inappropriate behavior must first examine intention. Do you want to teach a new self-discipline skill or new way of acting? Are you tempted to retaliate to get rid of frustration? Youth will recognize our positive intentions in *approach, communication,* and *attitude.* When our *approach* is positive, we help the child's self-esteem to remain intact. We do not demean ourselves by using correction that leaves us with a lessened sense of dignity. When our *communication* is positive, we...

- Start the conversation with a greeting.
- Give a simple directive to see if the person is willing to work with us (e.g. "Let's sit down").
- Assure the person, "This will only take a minute," and "I think you and I can work this out."
- Compliment the person on at least one behavior that demonstrates maturity.
- Describe in a calm voice, what we saw or heard. (e.g. "When I gave the assignment, you rolled your eyes, folded your arms, and said, 'I hate this!').
- With sincerity, point out the behavior that is not acceptable. (e.g. "When you respond like that, I felt disrespected... If you have an issue with the work, we can talk about it.").
- Ask for understanding (e.g. "Do you understand why we are having this discussion?" or Did I misunderstand your gestures or words.
- Ask for a demonstration or change (e.g. "What can I expect from you the next time an assignment is given?").
- Thank or compliment the student for working to resolve the problem. An effective confrontation should last no more than five minutes. If a discussion prolongs, agree to reschedule an extended meeting.

Keeping a positive *attitude* reminds us that the child who acts contrary is not a criminal. They remain a child, someone on the road to maturity. We can offer alternative ways of acting which will lead to the child becoming a more productive and loving individual. In addition, we can allow the child the time necessary to practice the new skill or behavior.

When confrontations are not viewed positively, discussions about disagreement can end in a battle-of-wills, preventing both adults and students from achieving a solution. Every Thursday, I assist sixth grade students with their homework. One day, I was checking Brandon's assignments when a form fell out of his notebook. I asked if I could look at the form. It read as follows:

Conduct Rules	Work/Study Rules
Control talking.	Be prepared and organized.
Control your actions.	Stay on task.
Own your choice.	Complete and turn in assignments.
Treat all people with respect.	Take responsibility for your learning.
Follow directions.	Get parent signature on weekly reports.

I found it strange that such a list would be given out in the second semester of the school year and that many of the rules were actually skills. "Mr. Smith just made up that list," said Brandon. "Was it because the class wasn't following the rules?" I asked. "No, it was because he couldn't handle us... If he writes down our name, we have to stay in at recess." I asked how many students stayed in class that day. "Almost half the class," Brandon reported. "We don't care about recess anyway. It's only ten minutes long and it was cold outside." When I suggested that the students behave better to avoid missing recess, Brandon responded, "Naw, he's not a good teacher. We just hope we don't have him again next year."

In this stalemate, the children did not view the problem as a shared responsibility. Behavior is unlikely to change when students are unable or unwilling to understand the problem from their teacher's point of view. The class spent little or no time discussing classroom rules. Students were not invited to identify the procedures they would need to follow; therefore, they did not take ownership. The students lacked motivation to learn, had not established a rapport with the teacher and eventually mutual respect was lost.

A word of caution when working with adolescents: If teens feel like adults do not value their input, they may be unwilling to resolve mutual problems. On the other hand, even if they feel valued and are able to resolve problems, adolescents may grumble and complain to their peers. Adults and students need to be mindful of paying restitution as an important part of problem solving. We must remember and teach it is okay to disagree. Disagreements do not define one person as right and the other wrong. We can agree to disagree while retaining respect and trust.

People in conflict tend to resort to their most basic and comfortable stances. If our strongest tendencies are to dominate a situation, we may view problems as a competition that we need to win. If we don't like conflict and disagreement, we may give up our positions and accommodate the other or avoid working toward a solution. Compromise and collaboration are the two best postures people can take to resolve problems. When we compromise, both parties listen, negotiate, win some, and lose some in the outcome. When we collaborate, both parties identify areas of agreement and disagreement, look for alternatives, and mutually agree on solutions.

The Case of the Missing Donuts

Two sophomores and a senior were caught taking donuts from a food tray for guests who were to visit the school. They decided to own-up to what they had done and went to talk to the teacher who had prepared the food. The teacher knew all three young men had completed a full year's course on self-discipline. She also knew they had trained to resolve problems of mutual concern.

After the initial greetings and handshakes, the teacher turned to the senior and said, "Tell me what happened."

The senior, with a flair for drama, said, "Oh, that French roast coffee you put out smelled so good, I was lured to the window. When I saw the donuts, temptation got the better of me and I took a few. But I am here to tell you I am sorry and I'll never do it again."

Without reacting to what the senior had said, the teacher turned toward the two sophomores and said, "What is your story?"

The first replied, "Well, we were on our way over to eat a donuts too, but when the senior was caught even though we didn't take any of the donuts, we were blamed for taking them too."

The teacher took a moment to distinguish between feeling and facts. In a calm voice, she thanked the young men for owning up to the problem, then asked how they would make restitution.

"Excuse me?" said the senior.

"How will you pay back what you took?" replied the teacher. "You just ate part of the breakfast I had prepared for my guests; I'd like you to replace what you took."

The senior said, "I can't do that. We're not allowed off campus during the school day."

The sophomores jumped in with a suggestion. "Can he replace the donuts with cookies from the school vending machines?"

Pleased, the teacher nodded. "I can live with that. I'd like you to do that as soon as possible. Is this agreeable to you?"

The senior shook his head reluctantly. "Yeah, I guess that would be fine."

The teacher continued, "Can we all agree that this conversation is over and will not be repeated?" She shook hands with all three of the students and thanked them for their help. She did not pass judgment or blame, but simply focused on the problem and its solution.

> "Respect for others entails having an essentially welcoming attitude toward the words they address to us. This means, among other things, that contradicting for its own sake should be banned as utterly uncivil. There are two fundamental abilities to cultivate in order to be agreeable in conversation: The ability to consider that you might be wrong. The ability to admit that you don't know.
>
> Choosing Civility, P.M. Forni, p. 89

More Confrontation Tips

How can I confront inappropriate behavior without sounding defensive or threatening?

- Gain control of your emotions, especially your voice.
- Realize you cannot change anyone's behavior – you can prompt, give choices, request change, teach, and then have someone practice a skill.
- Say what you saw or heard. Don't assume you know what really took place.
- Say what you think the other person might be thinking, and then check it out for accuracy.

Should inappropriate behavior be confronted publicly or privately?

- Recognize the need for short-term action to end a disruption or disagreement and long-term action in which you discuss the inappropriate behavior and/or teach an alternative way of responding/reacting.
- In school, the entire class is aware that a student has acted inappropriately. When an adult does not take action, the behavior will most likely be repeated. Any interaction should allow the leaner to keep his/her self-esteem intact.

If a situation involves a student in another classroom who I have a rapport with, should I tell the other teacher I want to handle the problem or would they feel I was overstepping boundaries?

- Always *ask* rather than *tell* another teacher.
- Describe what you intend to do.
- Report how the confrontation evolved.
- Ask for feedback from the teacher.
- If your plan is successful, share the action with other teachers who might also have difficult with the student.

CHAPTER 18

The Skill of Initiating Solutions to Problems

 The skill of initiating solutions is shown here in a drawing of a clockwise spiral. This Tibetan sign for potential power symbolizes the action or movement that occurs when we take the risk to initiate a solution to resolve a problem.

*When we **TAKE THE INITIATIVE TO SOLVE A PROBLEM,***

*We **WAIT** until we notice that a problem exists.*

*We **THINK**: How can I state the problem so others will understand it? What is my plan for resolving the problem?*

*We **ACT**: We make the first move to resolve the issue.*

A cartoon pictures a seven-year-old sitting at the table finishing his homework. His mother tells him she wants help with tasks as soon as he completes his work. The boy responds with a long sigh. "What's wrong?" asks his mother. "I'm getting discouraged," he says. "Every year brings more responsibility and I'm finding it hard to deal with what I've got now."

To contrast the seven-year-old's disappointing revelation, is the story of two second graders who willingly took on more responsibility by writing a note to schedule an appointment with their principal. They showed up at the appointed time, eager to talk. When the principal asked, "What's on your mind?" the first student said, "We are here to initiate a solution to a problem." The second student declared, "We noticed that there are broken swings on the playground where the new first graders play." The principal listened and thanked them. Later, she told me, "I treated their problem the same way I would treat a more serious problem." She asked the girls to do some fact-finding and count the number of swings that needed replacement. As soon as the principal had the information, she notified maintenance and had the swings repaired. At the next school assembly, she acknowledged the second graders and recognized them for having practiced a high-level self-discipline skill. When children learn the 15-skills framework, they begin to practice the higher-level skills at earlier ages.

> "There is no doubt in my mind that assertiveness is part of the set of quiet but powerful interactive skills of civility."
>
> Choosing Civility, P.M. Forni, p. 111

Responding to Problems

Adults need to be mindful of the times they rush to fix problems rather than let children grapple with the complexity of a childhood issue. Adults can propose three types of responses to a problem. Children may be most familiar with an *aggressive* response, in which the action is hostile or violent. When upset, the immediate and impulsive reaction might be to strike out. This response is not acceptable but should be acknowledged since children witness real life instances.

If children have limited experience initiating solutions to their problems, they may not want to act. A *passive* response is to walk away, just think about the problem, make light of it, or do something only indirectly related to the problem. Adults can encourage *assertive* responses, in which individuals act in a calm deliberate manner and communicate their concerns while working toward a solution.

Jim Fay, the well-known educational consultant and author of *Love and Logic,* suggests adults use the following guidelines to help children take the initiative to resolve problems:

Honor the fact that they have a problem: "That is a problem."

Inquire: "Have you thought about how you will fix it?"

Offer Alternatives: "Would you like me to tell you what others in your situation have done?"

162

Honor the response. If they say "No," let them think about it on their own. If they say "Yes," give them at least three action steps they could take similar to the following:

- Suggest an aggressive approach before ruling it out as an alternative.
- Suggest a passive approach because that is always an option when children are not ready to make the first move.
- Suggest an assertive response developmentally appropriate for the child (1995).

After this discussion, give the child time to think about workable solutions. Check back to discover what plan of action they have decided to take. One rule to apply to all solutions is, "You cannot fix a problem by making a problem for anyone else."

One sunny Saturday I was working in the yard along with most of my neighbors. Six-year-old Matthew was playing in his yard. It soon became apparent that Matthew's ball had rolled under my 25-foot evergreen tree. Matthew did what a six-year old does when he has a problem. He whined about his problem to my neighbor. I watched my neighbor quickly retrieve the ball for Matthew and send him on his way. I was disappointed that Matthew did not have a chance to initiate a solution to his problem.

As luck would have it, a half-hour later my doorbell rang. There stood Matthew. He told me his ball once again had rolled under my tree. I was thrilled! I would not deprive him of a chance to work out his own problem. I said, "Gosh, Matthew, that sounds like you have a problem. Have you thought about how you will fix it?"

With a straight face, he looked at me and, pointing to the neighbor's house, said, "Should I go get that lady and ask her to get it for me?"

Encouraging him, I replied, "Oh, you could, but she did the work last time and it really is your problem. Can you think of anything else that might work?"

He looked me up and down and said, "You could go change your clothes and go get it?"

Trying hard not to laugh, I said, "I could, but then I would be doing all the work. Can you think of something we can do together to help with your problem?"

Matthew thought, then said, "If you hold the branches, I'll crawl under and get the ball." I told him that was a great solution and the two of us left to retrieve his ball.

Vocabulary Starters

These vocabulary starters encourage children to think about solutions:

"Let's explore the alternatives."
"Put yourself in my place."
"Can we live with the things we cannot change?"
"Can you help me understand your reasons?"
"Is there a solution we haven't thought about yet?"
"Should we ask other people for some ideas?"
"How can we resolve this so we both can come out winners?"
"Thank you for making the first move to resolve this issue."

Initiating Solutions in the Middle Grades

Even if children in elementary school have had practice taking responsibility for solving their problems, pre-teens and teens will find this Generative skill challenging to demonstrate. When faced with an immediate personal decision, adolescents will often rely on feelings before intellect. They may know better but act contrary to that knowledge. At times, the school administrator may need to demonstrate taking the initiative to resolve problems.

An Example:

Librarian Carol Wilson complained to the principal one day that one of her fifth-grade classes had been rude to her. When Carol told them they were too noisy and that she couldn't stand it, one of the boys spoke up and said, "Yes, you can stand our noise. You're paid to do that."

The principal asked Carol, "What has been the history of your relationship with this class?"

Carol explained that several of the students challenged her on a regular basis and when they were not on the same page, she felt like a failure.

The principal suggested that Carol monitor her manner of speaking to the children to be sure *she* was respectful in her words. She offered to go into the classroom and talk to the students, warning Carol that this move was risky because the students may say things that she might not like to hear. In addition, the fifth graders might conclude Carol was unable to handle the class. Carol was willing to take the risk, so that afternoon the principal spoke to the fifth graders.

She told them she was concerned about some things that were happening. She was going to speak to them for a few minutes and then wanted to hear their observations about the situation. Heading directly to the problem, the principal said, "I know that someone in this classroom said that Mrs. Wilson was paid to put up with anything students wanted to shout and I want you to know I strongly disagree." She spoke briefly about authority, explaining to them that as a principal and as a teacher/librarian respectively, their job was to help, guide, and facilitate learning. Whether they should be respected depends on several factors.

She asked if Mrs. Wilson was a good role model for them. Students responded in the affirmative saying she was friendly and she spoke nicely to them. She was always ready for them when they came into the library. Then she asked if Mrs. Wilson acted like she had experience and knew how to run the library.

The students gave examples that highlighted Mrs. Wilson's ability to help them locate materials and answer their questions. Mrs. Wilson verified that although she was new to the school, she was not a new librarian and had seven years of experience.

The principal ended her five-minute talk by reiterating the problem. "I think the remark was out of line and whoever made the remark can apologize. You and Mrs. Wilson have a good working relationship and I'd like to see that continue."

165

Mrs. Wilson thanked the principal for visiting. She then gave each of the students a 3x5 index card and asked them to sign the card and write their insights and opinions regarding the incident. The cards would be given directly to the principal and later the principal would debrief with Mrs. Wilson.

In this example, the principal showed the students that while they have a right to their opinions, they have a responsibility to become informed. No adult will be idle when a student uses an abusive tone or gesture with the intention of disrespecting another person. Teachers too will be counseled to show respect to students in their words and actions as the Administrator takes the initiative to lead.

Helping Pre-teens Take the Initiative:

Teens and pre-teens frequently justify actions by describing how many of their peers engage in the activity. "Everyone's doing it," is a familiar cry. Adults must challenge adolescents to think about their knowledge, experience, and value systems. A good question is, "What would you do if half of your friends engaged in an action and the other half did not?"

Some students will only take the initiative and seek help if personally invited by the teacher. When there is a problem, it takes courage and practice to make the first move. The following principles will function as a guide when practicing this skill:

Go to the source of a problem.
Talk it through with a neutral person.
Make an appointment when you need to speak with someone.
Put what you want to say in writing.
Be willing to change your point of view if new evidence comes to light.
Keep the attitude that different viewpoints are both natural and healthy.

Discuss with students how difficult it is to be the first to act when there is a problem. Assign the task of writing or illustrating a time when a problem could not be solved because no one was willing to make the first move. Ask for a few volunteers to share their stories or illustrations. After listening, invite students to list three conditions that will help someone make the first move and three conditions that make it difficult. Challenge students to look for opportunities to initiate solutions during the week and report back what they observed.

A fifth grader reported that she was having difficulty with a friend. She needed time to put her thoughts into words, so she decided to write her friend a letter. She was able to make the first move to initiate a solution when she wrote this letter.

Dear Natalie,

> When we first met you were nice to me. You listened when I said something. When I told you something, you didn't laugh and go tell everyone and you weren't always saying "I don't like this about you." But things have changed and lately you've been making me mad. You keep saying things like "No offense… but," or "Not to be mean… but," and it hurts my feelings. Most of the time the only reason I don't walk home from school with you is because you get me so mad, I'm afraid I'll say something drastic or you will hurt me so badly that I will go home crying. You don't seem to notice or care that you're hurting my feelings so, until you change, I'm no longer your friend.
>
> P.S. If you have anything to say, please just write me a letter since I'll be gone this weekend.

People who are neither taught nor motivated to practice the skill of initiating solutions exhibit these behaviors:

- Fail to own behavioral choices.
- Do not know effective practices to use when taking the first step.
- Avoid confrontations.
- Cannot identify resource persons who could help solve a problem.
- Do not critique solutions to learn how to be more effective.
- Fail to help others unless prompted to do so.

Strategies to Learn How to Make the First Move

Explore the elements of skill 13 by discussing how to handle problems. Try this game: Write each of the phrases below on a slip of paper and put the slips into a container.

When four to six people have gathered, invite the youngest person to pull a slip from the container and finish the sentence. Allow discussion to flow freely before moving to the next person in the group.

The most difficult problem I have had to face is...
When I face problems I usually...
When I am angry I usually...
It can be difficult to make the first move when there are problems because...
When someone comes to me with a problem I...
The easiest problem I ever had to fix was...
One tip I have learned about taking the first step to resolve a problem is...
If you have a problem never ...

End the discussion by inviting each person to tell one thing they learned about themselves or a member of the group. Engage students in discussion using issues that might be of concern to the class.

Which of these six problems do you consider the most serious for a student? Why?

a) Disrupting class so others cannot learn.
b) Inability to remember to bring home books needed to do homework.
c) Not studying for tests and getting below average grades.
d) Being offered drugs when you don't use them.
e) Cyberbullying.
f) Being harassed by a member of the class.

If you had a friend who had the problem what three ideas would you suggest for fixing it?

Would your friend need other students or persons to do anything to help them with this problem? What could they do to help?

If a plan was put into action and there were no results, what would be the next step?

Do you think if one person changes the way they do something, it will cause a change in another person?

How easy or difficult do you think it is to initiate a solution to the problem you selected?

The acronym IDEA is useful when a person wants to initiate a solution to a problem or root out negative behavior.

I	Identify the problem	What happened/is happening? What did you do? What can you do? Is it helping you and/or others?
D	Develop a Plan to Fix the Problem	What change can you make in your behavior? Can another person help you? What do you need to get out of this problem? What will happen if you do not make the first move?
E	Execute the Plan	After designing a plan, put it into effect immediately. Stick to your new plan for at least two weeks before making changes.
A	Analyze the Results	After two weeks, look at what is happening. Ask if your plan is helping or making things worse. Solicit additional help if you are unable to initiate a solution to your problem.

Think before you decide to act. Reflect on these questions:

- Does this person's behavior affect me directly? Has it happened more than once and is it likely to happen again?
- Is this a good time to deal with the issue?
- Are my feelings about the issue neutral so I don't act out of anger, jealousy, revenge, et cetera?
- Would this issue resolve itself?
- Am I the best person to address the issue?
- Can I think of someone else who might be better at confronting the issue?
- Am I ready to let this matter drop once I've expressed my feelings and asked for what I need or want?

A Skill Code Saves the Day

The staff at a private school developed a behavior code at the beginning of the school year. All teachers agreed that they would model the self-discipline skills by demonstrating specific actions. Items on the list included:

Listening	We will use the steps of listening when we are in faculty meetings.
Follow Instructions	We will follow the procedures outlined in the policy handbook.
Ask Questions	We will ask questions rather than assume we know answers to issues.
Social Skills	We will greet all faculty members using a professional title.
Cooperation	We will look for opportunities to teach parents about self-discipline.
Communication	We will speak supportively about the school, students, staff, and policies.
Resolving Problems	We will be constructive when we need to complain.
Initiating Solutions	We will go to the source of a problem to resolve concerns.
Distinguishing Facts from Feelings	We will refrain from solving problems when our emotions are too strong.
Sacrifice/Be of Service	We will take the extra time needed to help students or staff members.

A member of the staff typed the completed list, purchased simple frames, and gave each teacher a framed copy of the behavior code. This simple activity built a collaborative spirit among the staff.

In March, Mrs. Abts, one of the fifth-grade teachers, found out from a co-worker that a peer had been talking about her in the faculty room. The comments were innocent but inaccurate and Mrs. Abts was upset no one came to her to verify the information. No one likes conflict yet, she knew she had to confront her peer.

At the end of the day, she took down the framed behavior code and marched down the hall to speak to the teacher who had made the comments. After greeting the teacher, she asked, "Is this a good time for us to visit for a few minutes?" When the peer said it was, Mrs. Abts started by showing her the code. "We agreed to model the self-discipline skill of initiating solutions to problems by going to the source of the problem and that's why I am here. I need to talk with you about what I heard."

Both teachers felt better when the confrontation was over. Mrs. Abts confessed this was the first time she had the courage to confront a peer.

The other teacher also felt as if this was a first. "Last year when things like this happened, we just whispered behind people's backs, leaving everyone with a very unprofessional and uncomfortable feeling," her peer admitted. "I'm sorry. I know this wasn't easy for you. I'm glad you confronted me, because I was wrong in not coming to you first."

Sample Code: Highlighting the Skill of Resolving Problems

1. We will be consistent in handling challenging situations. Consistency can mean all teachers will have the same consequences for rule infractions. It can also mean all teachers will act when there is a rule infraction, but what they do may differ depending upon the circumstances.

2. All staff will maintain a posture of approachability when students, parents, other staff report problems. This posture will be evident in tone, language, and an attitude that welcomes problems as opportunities for growth and change.

3. When students complain about other teachers, we will ask, "Have you spoken to the teacher?" "Do you want help to know how to begin a conversation?" We will set a date for the student to report back to us their progress.

4. If there are rules we cannot accept or think should be changed, we will work to revise the school handbook at the appropriate time.

5. When we need to confront someone, we will use skill language to describe unacceptable behavior.

CHAPTER 19

The Skill of Distinguishing Facts from Feelings

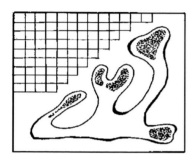 To be the best in our relationships with others, we must learn the skill of separating fact from feeling. This illustration shows fact represented by hard-edged black and white, closed forms or shapes. Feelings are shown in the contrasting gray, free-form shapes.

When we DISTINGUISH FACTS FROM FEELINGS,

We WAIT until we have neutralized strong emotions.

We THINK: What name can I put on my feelings? What are the facts?

How are my feelings affecting both my body and mind?

We ACT: We list the facts and our feelings to get an accurate picture of the situation.

Yareth's Story

Ten-year-old Yareth often received the hand-me-downs of the family. The last one she received was a computer, but it didn't have Internet access, e-mail, or instant messaging, a big part of a fourth grader's social life.

One Sunday while scanning the local newspapers, Carla and her husband saw a collection of relatively inexpensive laptops. They wondered if they should purchase one for Yareth so she would no longer ask to use theirs. That afternoon they went to the computer store with their son Torwin. When Torwin realized the computer was for his sister, he seemed unusually quiet. Carla asked if he was upset. "Well, when I turned 13, you gave me my computer for my birthday. You told me, 'You only turn 13 once.' I don't think she should get her own computer at ten years old."

Carla's husband told him that Yareth was using their computer too much and they were unable to access it for personal or professional work. Computers were cheaper now and they could get her a new one at less cost than adding on to her old one. This answer quieted him, but Carla could tell it didn't satisfy him.

That night Carla and her husband discussed Torwin's concerns. Maybe the answer wasn't to buy Yareth a new computer, but rather set the limits of time and restrict access to certain Internet sites. This might also show her brother that the gift on his thirteenth birthday was indeed special, a response to him that they had listened, acknowledged, and respected his feelings and opinions.

They decided not to purchase the computer. When school was out, instant messaging took a back seat to bike-riding and swimming. In the end, they allowed Yareth to use the parents' computer 45 minutes per day to check e-mail and play a few games. Carla and her husband got their work done and their son seemed to be very happy.

Facts and Feelings

A fact is something that has occurred or is certain to occur that can be proved with evidence. A feeling elicits a partly-mental, partly-physical response. Feelings involve pleasure or pain, attraction toward or movement away from an object, person, or event. A balance between facts and feelings helps us make good decisions and lead happier lives. When we experience conflicting feelings, we know our heads and our hearts are trying to find that balance.

Performing the skill of distinguishing fact from feeling is not a matter of letting go of feelings; rather, we use our feelings to enhance factual outcomes. If we only act from feelings, we can jump to wrong conclusions, make false assumptions, or cause needless worry. If we only consider the facts, we are unlikely to discover the impact or meaning of events for ourselves and others. We teach students to distinguish facts from feelings so they can:

- Accurately name feelings or describe how they are feeling.
- Trust both comfortable and uncomfortable feelings.
- Combine feelings with facts in order to make sound decisions.
- Reflect on personal choices.
- Avoid overreacting to minor incidents.
- Identify cues that indicate they are experiencing mixed emotions.
- Accurately report the facts so they can be objective.

Naming Feelings

Feelings most generally localize somewhere in one's body. We can put a name to that feeling when we realize how it affects both body and mind. We can learn to acknowledge and accept comfortable and uncomfortable feelings. We can realize feelings are neutral and avoid blaming ourselves for the ways we feel.

To help young children identify where feelings localize in their body, we use a checklist to identify the strength of feelings. Some questions to ask are, "Where do you feel anger? Do you feel it in your head, your eyes, cheeks, mouth, throat, your hands, your chest, your stomach, your legs, your feet or somewhere else?" Then ask, "What does it feel like?"

One child responded, "I feel the anger in my eyes. It feels like my eyes have x-ray vision and I can see through things." One child stated, "I feel excited in my stomach. It feels like there is popcorn in there bouncing up and down." Another said, "Excitement spreads throughout my entire body and I feel electric." Children begin to understand the uniqueness of feelings when several children describe the same feeling differently.

Mixed Emotions

We teach children the way to deal with strong or mixed emotions. Using the imagery of a step ladder, the words MIXED EMOTIONS are placed on the center rung. Below the rung are listed non-productive actions individuals might use when they are unable to identify and cope with their strongest emotions. Non-productive actions include teasing others, name calling, using inappropriate language, yelling, damaging or stealing property, hurting oneself or others physically. All these actions may and can occur and indicate the individual could not stop, wait and think before acting.

175

When people are experiencing strong or mixed emotions, they need space to regain a balance of feeling. Alternative responses to running from emotion or freezing with inactivity are listed above the center rung and include:

- Calm your mind and muscles.
- Count to ten before saying anything.
- *Wait* until the strong feelings have settled down.
- Talk to a friend or adult.
- Name and describe feelings.
- Make a drawing that represents what you are feeling.
- Use the phrases, "I have mixed emotions and do not know how I feel," and "My emotions are too strong now, I need time to think."

Sometimes taking a break is the best way to move the focus from feelings to fact. You can take a walk, clear your head, use deep-breathing exercises, or meditate. The intensity of the emotional reaction can determine the length of a break.

Use Stories and Poetry to Gain Empathy

Empathy comes from being able to see things from another person's perspective. Empathy can help one move from strong feelings to a fact-based decision. Most decisions affect other people in some way. To make a good decision, look at the facts of its outcome on others and act in a manner that is best for everyone. With older students, sharpen the skill of distinguishing fact from feeling by discussing situations such as the following:

One of the hardest tests of the school year will be at the end of the week. Bob has been a good student, but he is worried he has forgotten information, or won't do as well as his parents expect. The pressure to achieve good grades is high for Bob. Last evening, Bob's friend Jim phoned to say his older brother found a copy of the standardized test from last year, the same test for this year. Jim invited Bob to study with him so they could be sure to get a good score. Bob *felt* good grades would really make his parents happy, which made him consider cheating with his friend Jim.

After presenting this scenario, teachers instruct students to answer questions:

- Make a list of the *facts* and *feelings* Bob might be experiencing.
- If you were in Bob's shoes, what would you do?
- If Bob were your friend and came to you to talk about his mixed emotions, what would you tell him?
- Create a role play for each situation.

The Empty Pot

Another terrific story that can help students reflect on facts and feelings is *The Empty Pot* by Demi. In this Chinese tale, an emperor who is growing old decides to leave his throne to someone worthy, someone who shares his love for flowers. So, he designs a plan. He gives one flower seed to each child in his kingdom and tells them, "Take this seed and cultivate it for one year. At the end of the year, whoever can show me their best, the fruits of their labor, shall succeed me on the throne."

One young man named Ping had a reputation for growing beautiful plants. When given his seed, he cupped it in his hands and carefully carried it all the way home. Ping cultivated the soil, planted the seed, watered it, and tended it carefully, but nothing grew. As time passed and still nothing grew, Ping repotted the seed in new soil. Once again, nothing grew.

The day arrived when all the children were to return to the emperor. Large, beautiful plants of every color, smell, and shape rose above the children's pots. Ping was not excited. He went to his father and said "Father, I do not want to go today. I am ashamed. The other children will laugh at me because for once, I couldn't get a flower to grow." Ping's father said, "Son, you did your best and your best is good enough to present to the emperor."

Holding the empty, large pot in his hands, Ping went to the palace. What a splendid sight the emperor saw! Magnificent flowers were all over the courtyard. The emperor looked at each flower slowly, one by one. He did not say a word, nor did he smile. Finally, he came to Ping. Ping hung his head in shame. He was scared and expected punishment. The emperor said, "Tell me about your seed, boy." Ping started to cry as he explained, "I took the seed you gave me and I planted it. When it didn't grow, I repotted it and gave it care once again. I tended it all year long, but nothing grew. So today, I had to bring an empty pot. It was the best I could do."

When the emperor heard this, he put his arm around Ping and shouted, "I have found him! I have found the one person worthy of being an emperor!" Then he looked at all the other children and said, "Where you children got your seeds, I do not know. For the ones that I gave out had all been boiled. It was impossible for them to grow." When the story ends, students discuss the facts of the story as well as the feelings that Ping might have experienced. They also discuss deeper questions. How did the children get their seeds? Why might the emperor have been displeased with them? What circumstances tempt you to distort the truth?

Poems by Christine Ryktarsyk

My Secret Fear

No one knows my secret fear
So please don't tell a soul.
I have this terrible, nagging fear
That I'll fall down a hole.

The hole will be dark and deep and dank,
And I will fall and fall,
Picking up slimy, creepy critters
Whenever I brush a wall.

When I finally, finally reach the bottom
I'll hit with a deafening thud!
And when I try to stand up, I'll find that I can't
'Cause I'm up to my hips in mud!

I'll rock and I'll jump and I'll squirm all around,
Trying to get myself free,
But in the end, I'm afraid it will be
The dark hole, the mud, and... me.

Why Do I Have to Eat Breakfast? (A Breakfast Rap)

Does your stomach ever growl
When you're sitting in school?
But you can't grab a sandwich
'Cause it's against the rules.

So you sit there feeling hungry
And you're starting to feel weak.
You wish you'd eaten breakfast
Or drank some juice, at least.

Your stomach's very empty,
No fuel to feed your mind.
Can't listen to the teacher.
Just food you want to find.
Not getting any work done.
Don't like the way you feel.

Now you know...
Don't come to school
Before you eat a meal.

178

Overreactions

Distinguishing fact from feeling is especially difficult when feelings change rapidly. There are many opportunities when students' feelings cause them to overreact due to sensitivity and a lack of confidence. Overreaction of one or two students can affect the entire class.

Here are just a few occasions when children and teens have trouble separating fact from feeling:

- When placed in a group of peers with which they are uncomfortable

- When tests are announced

- When the schedule is disrupted and they must give up an activity they really like

- When they don't get the grade they had anticipated

- When they are corrected in public

- If too much homework is assigned

- When they have a substitute teacher

- When the answer to a request is "No"

- If they are asked to watch a younger sibling and they had other plans

- When money is not given for items the teen wishes to purchase

- When topics are discussed that they are not comfortable talking about

Overreacting is an emotional response out of proportion to the situation. External overreactions include shouting, slamming things, making unwanted noises, using inappropriate words, et cetera. Sometimes people internalize the emotional response. *DWP* teachers instruct students to get into the habit of *waiting* before responding. To diminish the overreaction, we say, "I'm going to ask you to do or say something that you might not like. Please think about it before responding."

We all need to notice when we overact and ask ourselves if the incident will be important tomorrow. If the answer is no, then whatever we are reacting to in the moment isn't a big deal.

At home or in a classroom, when adults are irritated by a child's actions, they may feel angry, annoyed, or frustrated. Like children, adults often overact when intimidated or threatened by feelings. The adult can ask themselves questions to integrate their emotions with the facts.

"What is the best thing for me to do that will help the child?"

"Can I deal with this now, or do I need time to think about the situation?"

"Is there an immediate temporary or long-term action I can take?"

"Is there a missing self-discipline skill that I can begin to teach the child?"

Children will learn to separate fact from feeling as they watch adults practice the skill. Here are behaviors adults can model to show students ways to distinguish fact from feeling:

- Allow students to see you get legitimately angry or passionate about issues of injustice, inequality, lack of integrity, et cetera.

- Be calm in stressful situations.

- Remain neutral. Avoid reacting to feelings too strong to be tempered with the facts.

- Acknowledge that you will need time to think about a situation rather than react impulsively.

- Count to ten when you feel frustration building. Place your hands behind your back and take several deep breaths.

- Sit down so you do not appear to be overtaking the power of another. When you continue to stand are taller/bigger, students often feel they are in a win/lose situation.

- Avoid raising your voice and shouting, unless you must prevent an unsafe, illegal, or immoral action. Even in these matters, an adult who can separate fact from feeling and talk rationally about the situation will be a better mediator for the students.

- When children disagree with one another, or with you, provide them with a written plan of action or a reporting sheet to diffuse the emotion.

Matt's Story

Holy Rosary School had been teaching the 15 self-discipline skills for over seven years. Many of the students, who had begun in kindergarten, were now in the junior high. They had grown up practicing the skills and knew the skill language well. Together, the adults and students continued to work to demonstrate the skills in daily life.

One day, Matt, a junior high student, was sent to the office to visit the principal. This was Matt's third visit in less than two weeks and Principal Riggert was disappointed to see his return for disciplinary reasons.

Holy Rosary was exactly the type of school Matt needed because teachers wanted to see him succeed and Mrs. Riggert genuinely liked Matt despite his misbehavior. This third visit to the office meant she would have to give Matt a stronger consequence for his behavior. She would draw up a contract and place stipulations on his behavior if he wanted to stay at the school.

Matt, too, was disappointed in his behavior. He liked the adults in the school, especially the principal who he knew was trying to help him. He looked at his principal's face and very quietly said, "Mrs. Riggert, do you need some time to separate fact from feeling?"

Mrs. Riggert nodded. She noted how well the staff had taught Matt to recognize how his behavior affected other people. "Yes, Matt," she said. "In fact, I think you had better just take a seat and give me some time to figure out what I need to say to you."

How I Got My Children to Stop Arguing

by Lynn Murtagh

Three self-discipline skills are missing when children can't get along.

Social Skills: I taught my children that it is appropriate to use the same social skills with siblings as they do with their friends. I coached them to practice respectful morning and after-school greetings and to use good manners in their discussions with one another. I complimented them when I saw positive interactions.

Communication: I told my children that they could respect another's point of view even if they disagreed. Teasing, one-upping, and taunting are not appropriate forms of communication. Body language, tone, and gestures are as important as the spoken word. I repeated what a child said using the same negative tone and then modeled a better way to say things. When I was sure they understood the difference between positive and negative communication tones, I simply said, "Say the same thing again, but with a better tone." Or "Try again to say that without sarcasm." I insisted the children talk to one another when they had hurt or angry feelings. "Use words and tell your brother what you do not like."

Resolving Problems: Our ground rules in our home included: No hitting, name-calling, put-downs, or yelling. If any of these rules were not followed, I gave a verbal warning and, if necessary, a time-out. When caught in a conflict, I coached my children by asking them to think of three ways their problem could be solved. When they could not think of three different ways, I offered suggestions so they could learn there are many alternatives to violence and disrespect.

CHAPTER 20

The Skill of Serving Others

The small symbol in the lower right corner of the drawing is a rune, a character of an ancient alphabet. This particular rune named Ur or Uruz, means both strength and sacrifice. It is repeated here to form a radiant design to show how mastering the skill of sacrifice or service to others brings us out of ourselves and our own needs to consider those of others.

*When we **SACRIFICE OR SERVE OTHERS**,*

*We **WAIT** to have our needs or desires met while we put others' needs and desires first.*

*We **THINK**: What am I willing to let go of so life will be better for others?*

*We **ACT**: We choose a course of action that will be the best choice and move forward.*

Recently a group of fourth graders looked at a picture of a mother holding a small child. The picture was labeled "Making Sacrifices." Several children wanted to know, "What is a sacrifice?" The teacher explained: "It is when two or more valuable things are desired and only one of the items can be had... You give something up to gain something equally as good or better." She told them making a sacrifice can be difficult because you can't possibly have it both ways, so you must stop and think before deciding. The children thought about this together and came up with examples:

- "I wanted to buy something for myself, but I also needed the money to buy a gift for my sister."
- "The court ordered me to choose to live with Mom or Dad."
- "I had invitations from two different friends to do two different activities on the same day and I had to choose."

The children understood that by giving up something, they would gain something:

- "A sacrifice play in baseball allows another player to reach home plate or an extra base."
- "If I want to enjoy our family pet, I must take the time to feed and care for that pet."
- "When my Mom gave up sweets, she lost weight."

A week later, a fourth grader stayed in from recess to tell his teacher this story: "There are four of us in the neighborhood and we decided when we shoveled snow for the neighbors, we would save the money and give it to someone who needed it. We have 26 dollars in our box now and I just wanted you to know that."

The teacher complimented the boy and said, "You must feel very proud of the sacrifice you are making. Is this skill difficult for you?"

"Heck, no," said the boy. "In fact, I'm making another one right now."

"You are?" asked the teacher.

"Yes," the boy replied. "My class is out at recess and I'm in here telling you about the sacrifice I made."

We live in an age where self-esteem and self-expression are highly valued. But what a selfish world we would live in if we focused on ourselves to the exclusion of other human beings. We must ask ourselves if the happiness of others is important to us.

Primary children will understand this skill more from an adult's affect and manner of speaking than from a conceptual basis (e.g. "When you shared your cookie with Curt who did not have one, you made my heart feel really warm. You made a sacrifice and that is a very difficult skill for some people to practice.")

Primary children learn that when they choose to perform any self-discipline skill, there will be a benefit to themselves and others.

Children learn the Service to Others song, using the tune *Baa! Baa! Black Sheep.*

> Service to Others,
> What can I do?
> Give of my time.
> And spend it with you.
>
> Service to Others,
> What can it be?
> Give something special
> To you from me.
>
> Service to others
> What can I say?
> Ask the question,
> "Can I help you today?"

To make the concept of serving others concrete, each child is given an 8 ½ x11 inch sheet of paper and is told to print their names in the center of the circle. To self-assess, students write or draw a picture of a time when they acted kindly toward another. At the end of each day, a hole is punched in any quadrant where items have been recorded. When the paper is full, students receive a shiny piece of tissue paper to lay behind their circle. When held up to the light or posted in a window, the light of their good works shows through.

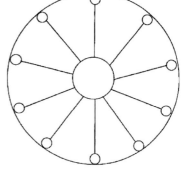

Students in grades three and four can understand this skill when we use terms that are familiar to them. To sacrifice means "Being Super Fair." Students brainstorm actions they consider to be Super Fair. Here are some simple actions children can do to practice the skill of serving others.

- Offer to explain assignments to a classmate who is ill.
- Ask a family member if you can help them with a chore.
- Volunteer as a family to help a neighbor.
- Perform an act of kindness, which draws as little attention to yourself possible.

Have you ever driven up to a fast food restaurant and been told by the attendant that your meal was paid for by the person ahead of you? Or maybe, you picked up the tab on lay-away items for someone during the holidays. The concept of "pay-it-forward" gained renewed interest when the movie of that same title came out in 2000. In the movie, a social studies teacher gives an assignment to his junior high school class - to think of an idea to make the world better. One young student creates a plan for "paying forward" favors. In doing so, he helps his struggling single-mother and starts a wave of human kindness. Children of all ages can grasp the concept of paying-it-forward as an example of service to others.

Why Teach Children to Serve Others?

Serving others connects you to people. It curbs self-centeredness and the "What's in it for me?" attitude. Service helps us view things from another person's perspective. It gives children an opportunity to move out of their comfort zones, instills a habit of volunteering, and can make the world a better place. Serving others is a life skill. To children, we explain 'sacrifice' generally as charity, to serve others, to help others, to give up our own interests and desires and to put others before ourselves. Vocabulary phrases that encourage people to practice the skill of sacrificing include:

- "What are you willing to give up?"
- "What will you gain?"
- "That action was 'super fair.'"
- "Not everyone will be able to practice the skill of sacrificing."
- "I need a volunteer."
- "The kind of volunteer I need is someone who won't get the giggles when they are in front of people, who likes to role play, who can take this task seriously."
- "This isn't a matter of fairness. I'm asking you to think about the needs of others now."

How Students Practice Sacrificing/Serving Others

Mary and Gene have two children. Both parents are professionals and have given the children learning opportunities since they were small. This year, when Mary asked her sixth-grader Sara

186

for suggestions on how she wanted to celebrate her birthday, Mary was surprised by her response. Instead of the traditional birthday party, Sara wanted to invite nine friends to take a trip to the Humane Society to visit and walk the animals. The invitation read, "No birthday gifts wanted. See attached list from the Humane Society's website and please bring a donation for an animal." The plan was to visit the animals and then all go to a movie.

The day was a huge success! The director of the shelter complimented the girls when they gave their gifts, took a group picture for their newsletter, and asked Sara if she wanted to write an article to accompany the picture. When it was time to leave the shelter, the girls asked, "Do we have to go to a movie?" The good feelings the girls experienced by giving of themselves at the shelter led them to forego the movie and instead go to a nearby restaurant so they could converse about the experience. The act of real giving evokes a sense of receiving.

One 17-year old told this story:

My parents gave birth to their fifth child and everyone in the family was thrilled. A special celebration to welcome this new child into the community was planned. The day chosen for the celebration turned out to be the day of the state championship basketball game. I was an important team player. I had responsibilities to the team and to my family. In discussing the matter with my mom, she understood my dilemma and said, "You must decide for yourself. You know how we feel and how your team will feel." I hated this choice!

In the end, she chose to play in the championship game. When the team won, she left their celebration to hurry home and take part in as much of the family celebration as possible.

People who make sacrifices often encounter dilemmas that involve their time, finances, values, or needs. They must compare the needs of others and decide what is best for the most people. Upon deciding and acting upon it, they focus on the satisfaction of their choice. They live with their decisions and avoid nurturing regrets. Lastly, they accept compliments that may come from others who appreciate what they have done.

Teens find it easy to *sacrifice* and *be of service* to friends. The challenge is to broaden their world view so they can take these skills into the community or show a generous attitude toward family members. Many schools include community service as part of their graduation requirements. Students who engage in service activities broaden their perspective by living in the shoes of others. This valuable skill leads many students to search for job opportunities that include giving back to the community.

When a group of eighth graders were learning about the self-discipline skill of serving others, their teacher introduced the custom called Otu'han, which means "giveaway." On certain special occasions, an honored member of the Lakota (Sioux) tribe gives away much of what he or she owns to other members of the tribe. Sometimes, the person gives away all their possessions. The practice stems from the Native American belief that all we have belongs to the Great Spirit and is meant to be shared with others.

The eighth graders drew up a list of principles to remind them of the components in this skill:

- I can try to notice when two valuable items come in competition. Example: I want to go out with my friends, but my Mom needs me to watch my baby brother.
- I can be mature and let go of thinking everything must be fair.
- I can perform acts of kindness not for a reward, but to think about other people.
- I can recognize that not everyone will choose to practice this skill. I might be the only one.
- When I volunteer, I will follow through with my commitment even if something more attractive comes up.
- When I think of the needs of others, I know that my needs may not get met.

Examples of people serving others are easy to find. Someone may uproot and move across country to be closer to aging parents and to care for them. People routinely visit nursing homes and socialize with strangers until they become friends. They donate their time, talent, and treasures to worthy causes. Adults can highlight such stories and point out how people often choose the greatest good.

The Last Word

Maimonides, a Jewish philosopher, observed people who performed acts of kindness. He noticed that not everyone gives with the same spirit of selflessness. He identified motives that people use when giving and called them The Eight Levels of Charity.

1. The highest form of charity is to help the poor become self-supporting by lending money, taking them into partnership, or giving them work until they no longer need to be dependent upon others, for in this way there is no loss of self-respect.
2. We can give without knowing to whom we are giving, and the recipient does not know from whom he received.
3. We can give in such a way that one knows to whom one gives, but the recipient does not know his benefactor.
4. We can give in such a way that the giver does not know to whom he or she is giving but the recipient does know his benefactor.
5. We can give directly to the person in need and do so before being asked to give.
6. We can give only after being asked.
7. We can give inadequately, but gladly and with a smile.
8. We can give but give unwillingly.

Christmas Giving

For about a year, Christopher, age ten, had been engaged in a school project in which students select an elderly person and become their pen pal. Throughout the year, Christopher exchanged cards and letters with Martha, an aging woman in a retirement home.

During the holidays, Christopher asked if he might visit Martha and meet her for the first time. My friend was excited about having the entire family make this visit as part of their holiday activities. They made gifts and bought fragrant soaps and other toiletries to give to Martha.

Though the parents shared in this project, the work of phoning, talking to Martha, and scheduling the visit was Christopher's job. One day before Christmas, he phoned the nursing home and asked for Martha's room number. He was surprised to hear she had moved to another room. Worried, he asked if she could still have visitors. Instead of answering his question, the receptionist put him through to Martha.

When Martha answered the phone Christopher said, "Merry Christmas, Martha. This is Christopher, your pen pal." Christopher had trouble hearing her reply. "What did you say, Martha? I couldn't quite get that." Eventually, they arranged a meeting.

Visiting Martha was a new experience for the entire family. His sister Anna, age six, sat quietly watching and observing. She intuitively knew something special was happening. Christopher held Martha's hand and told her about Christmas at his house. It was evident that Martha had suffered a mild stroke and had difficulty talking. The parents were mindful of Martha's energy level and kept the conversation light and easy.

The visit lasted 20 minutes. In that time, five people in the room engaged in a new level of sharing the holiday spirit. Anna summarized the impact of the visit as they walked to the car to head home. "I'm going to have a pen pal when I get in the fifth grade too, Mom."

"Just about the most important thing we do in life is interacting with other human beings. Shouldn't improving the quality of this interaction be at the top of our agendas? Being civil in our everyday lives is a time-tested way to bring about such improvement. A better quality of human interaction makes for a better life – a saner, more meaningful, healthier, and happier life. It is that simple. It is really that simple. All we have to do is stop, think about it and then act. The sooner the better."

Choosing Civility, P. M. Forni, p. 184

CHAPTER 21

60 Ways to Nurture Self-Discipline

Listening

1. Teach a child the six steps of listening (p. 41).
2. Compliment a child for listening. Tell them one or more steps of the skill they performed well.
3. Design a listening cue that will be helpful for all to use (p. 42).
4. Read a story or news article and then check for understanding (comprehensive listening). Ask for the listeners' evaluation of the article (critical listening).

Following Instructions

5. Ask someone for their focused listening before giving instructions.
6. Invite your child to follow three or more oral instructions.
7. Routinely ask: "Do you know what to do?" "Do you know how to do it?" "How much time will you have to complete the task?"
8. Help someone practice following verbal instructions. Use the 'stand up, sit down' exercise with the story "The Colorful Shoes,"(p. 52).

Asking Questions

9. Compliment a child by naming the criteria they used for an effective question (p. 60).
10. Defuse a prolonged debate by asking, "What do you think I will say?" or "I have been your teacher for ____ months; how do you think I will respond?" or "Why don't you have the last word on the subject?"
11. Place an object in a bag or box. Invite children to guess the object by asking questions about the shape, weight, size, color, et cetera.
12. Point out embarrassing questions others might ask and tell children why the questions are embarrassing.

Sharing: Time, Space, People, and Things

13. Make two paper space mats (legal size paper for mats on a table and newsprint for children sitting on the floor). Laminate the mats, punch holes at the top, and insert a string in each so the mat can hang behind a bedroom door. Invite children to use the mat to learn how to contain space (p. 68).
14. Divide your home or classroom into sections and assign people the task of caring for the space assigned.
15. Teach children how to get someone's attention when busy (p. 69).
16. Be mindful of the amount of personal time you share with each member of the family.

Using Social Skills

17. Review with children the social norms expected when greeting people.
18. Teach when it is appropriate to say "Excuse me" (p. 77).
19. Teach etiquette at the table (p. 79).
20. Discuss the different types of bullies with your children (p. 82).

Cooperating

21. Brainstorm activities the family might engage in during family night (p. 95).
22. Assign each child a few chores equal to their age (p. 97).
23. Hold a family or class meeting and discuss group concerns.
24. Celebrate family success stories giving credit where credit is due.

Understanding the Reasons for Rules

25. Adopt the three family rules listed on page (p. 102).
26. Teach the difference between an adult-imposed and a self-imposed consequence (p. 104).
27. Develop a list of Rights and Responsibilities for the home.
28. Make up a game and write the rules to the game before playing it.

Accomplishing Tasks Independently

29. Decide on a family tradition to celebrate each time a child turns 13.

30. Develop a pre-teaching checklist outlining tasks a babysitter will need to accomplish.
31. Write a family goal that passes the SMART test (p. 113).
32. Adopt the rhyme, "If your work is sloppy, you will recopy," and apply it to students' homework.

Exhibiting Leadership

33. Teach the hidden qualities of leaders to your family (p. 117).
34. Talk about mistakes as being an opportunity to learn.
35. Use the delegation form described on page 121 when delegating home tasks.
36. Discuss personal gifts and qualities of each member of the family. Try the exercise on page 122.

Communicating

37. Engage in a five-minute conversation with each child in your family. Describe for them what it was like the day they were born.
38. Teach children what the non-verbal actions of rolling eyes or flicking one's hair communicates to others.
39. Make your home a Put-Up rather than a Put-Down zone by intentionally saying two nice things about a person for every negative statement made.
40. Visit a relative and ask a child to intentionally use the acronym FORM to conduct a conversation (p. 129).

Organizing

41. Test each child to determine if they can tell time without the use of their phone or tablet.
42. When correcting a child deliberately switch the skill vocabulary when describing behavior to match the child's developmental stage.
43. Teach the meaning of impulse control and ask for examples of when it is necessary (p. 136).
44. Look for a disorganized area in the home, in which items have been placed randomly. Work together to organize the space.

Resolving Problems

45. Debrief with a child after they have been in time-out, using the questions on page (p. 151).
46. Draw up a family contract (sample on page 152).
47. Design a consequence card to use in the home (p. 153).
48. Honor children's problems. Ask them if they have ideas on how to fix problems. Make suggestions but let them decide on a solution that will not make a problem for anyone else.

Initiating Solutions

49. Teach children the difference between working with someone else to resolve a problem and taking the initiative to make the first move to resolve a problem.
50. Talk about the difference between Aggressive, Passive, and Assertive responses. Outlaw aggressive responses in the home (p. 162).
51. Compliment children who show initiative to fix things.
52. Use the acronym IDEA explained on page 169 to root out a bad habit.

Distinguishing Fact from Feeling

53. Teach young children how to describe their feelings. Use the checklist described on page 175.
54. Talk about mixed emotions and the benefit of waiting before acting during emotional times (p. 175).
55. Discuss the story "The Empty Pot" with children (p. 177).
56. Talk about times when it is easy to overreact because a situation is unexpected. (p. 179).

Sacrificing/Serving Others

57. Talk about times when two or more valuable choices compete and you must let go of one choice to achieve the other.
58. Decide as a family on a way to "pay it forward" in your community.
59. Volunteer as a family.
60. Discuss the quote attributed to Mark Twain: "Kindness is a language which the deaf can hear and the blind can see."

References

American Academy of Pediatricians (AAP). 2018. "Pediatricians' Group Takes Strong Stance against Spanking, Yelling at Children." *Cook Children's Newsroom.* Accessed January 6, 2020. https://www.checkupnewsroom.com/pediatricians-group-takes-strong-stance-against-spanking-yelling-at-children/

Appelo, Jurgen. 2015. The Negotiation Training Experts Offers Negotiation sources on (www.negotiations.com.) "The 7 Levels of Delegation." Accessed February 25, 2020. https://medium.com/@jurgenappelo/the-7-levels-of-delegation-672ec2a48103.

"Banh Chung Banh Day – A New Year Story for Tet by ATG." *Against the Grain Productions: One voice. many stories.* Accessed January 6, 2020. http://againstthegrainproductions.com/?s=a+new+year+story

Ballard, Elizabeth Silance. 1995. "Three Letters from Teddy." *A 2nd Helping of Chicken Soup for the Soul.* Deerfield Beach, FL: Health Communications.

Bisenius, James Patrick. 2001. "Bully-Proofing Youth." Accessed January 6, 2020. https://www.youtube.com/watch?v=embHq6E2A38.

Bisenius, James Patrick. 2020. *Bully Proofing Youth.* Accessed January 6, 2020. http://bullyproofingyouth.com.

Boller, Paul, Jr. 1996. *Presidential Anecdotes.* 2nd edition. U.S.A.: Oxford University Press.

"Bloom's Taxonomy." *Center for Teaching.* Accessed January 26, 2020. https://cft.vanderbilt.edu/guides-sub-pages/blooms-taxonomy/

Boys Town Contributor. (2019, September 17). Boys Town: Saving Children, Healing Families. 2019. "From Father Flanagan to the Boys Town Education Model." Accessed January 22, 2020. https://www.boystown.org/blog/Pages/100-years-of-bt-schools-and-teaching-philosophy.aspx

Boys Town: Saving Children, Healing Families. (n.d.). "The Writings of Father Flanagan." Accessed January 22, 2020. https://www.boystown.org/about/father-flanagan/Pages/father-flanagan-quotes.aspx.

Caron, Christina. 2018. "Spanking Is Ineffective and Harmful to Children, Pediatricians' Group Says." *The New York Times*. (2018, November 5). Accessed January 6, 2020. https://www.nytimes.com/2018/11/05/health/spanking-harmful-study-pediatricians.html?action=click&module=RelatedCoverage&pgtype=Articles&region

CASEL. 2013. *Effective Social Emotional Learning Programs*. Accessed January 21, 2020. https://casel.org/core-competencies/

Coburn. Calum. 2019. "Negotiation Conflict Styles." Accessed March 3, 2020. www.negotiations.com/training/

Curwin, Richard L., Allen N. Mendler, and Brian D. Mendler. 1988. *Discipline with Dignity*. Virginia: Association for Supervision & Curriculum Development (ASCD).

Demi.1990. *The Empty Pot*. New York, NY: Henry Holt and Company.

Develop Education Skills. https://www.developeducationskills.com/shop/

Dreikurs, Rudolf, and Pearl Cassel. 1972. *Discipline Without Tears: What to do with children who misbehave*. New York, NY: Plume Books.

Duckworth, Angela L, and Martin E.P. Seligman. 2005."Self-Discipline Outdoes IQ in Predicting Academic Performance in Adolescents." *Psychological Science*. 16(2): 939-944. (2005, December 1). https://www.ncbi.nlm.nih.gov/pubmed/16313657

Duckworth, Angela. 2011. "Self-regulation strategies." *Educational Psychology*, 31(1):17-26.

Dunham, Meaghan. 2017. "What's in a Name? 21st Century Skills vs Social and Emotional Learning." *Aperture Education*. Accessed January 6, 2020. https://apertureed.com/whats-name-21st-century-skills-vs-social-emotional-learning/

Dunn, Rita & Kenneth. 1979. "Learning Styles/Teaching Styles: Should they... Can they... Be Matched?" *Educational Leadership*. The Association for Supervision and Curriculum Development. (January), 239-244.

Durlak, Joseph A. PhD, Celene E. Domitrovich PhD, and Robert P. Weissberg PhD. 2015. *Handbook of Social and Emotional Learning: Research and Practice.* Guilford Publications: New York, N.Y.

Fay, Jim and David Funk. 1995. *Teaching with Love and Logic.* USA: Love and Logic Press. https://wwwloveandlogic.com

"Following Instructions?" 2019. *Kid Sense.* Accessed January 26, 2020. https://childdevelopment.com.au/areas-of-concern/understanding-language/following-instructions/

Forni, P.M. 2002. *Choosing Civility: The 25 Rules of Considerate Conduct.* St. Martin Press. New York, NY.

"4 Cognitive Stages for Child Development." 2019. *Learning Rx: One-on-one Brain Training.* Accessed January 6, 2020. https://www.learningrx.com/4-cognitive-stages-for-child-development-faq.htm.

Good, Thomas, Bruce Biddle, and Jere Brophy. 1975. *Teachers Make a Difference.* New York, NY: Holt, Rinehart, and Winston.

Gordon, Thomas. 1989. *Teaching Children Self-Discipline.* New York, NY: Crown Publishers.

Griffin, Trudi. (2019, March 28). "How to Avoid Overreacting." *WikiHow.* Accessed January 6, 2020. https://www.wikihow.com/Avoid-Overreacting

Hawley, Robert, and Isabel L. Hawley. 1981. *Achieving Better Classroom Discipline.* USA: Education Research Associates.

Howard, Eugene R. *School Discipline Desk Book.* 1978. New York, NY: Parker Publishing.

Sheff, Donald. "Izzy, Did You Ask a Good Question Today?" *New York Times.* 1988, Jan. 19. Sect A 26. Accessed January 26, 2020.

https://www.nytimes.com/1988/01/19/opinion/l-izzy-did-you-ask-a-good-question-today-712388.html

Jones, Regina and Laurel N. Tanner. 1981. "Discipline: Claiming the Unclaimed Legacy." *Phi Delta Kappan.* (March): 494-497.

Julius, Dr. Gloria. (2019, January 18). "Encouraging Cooperation with Children." *Primrose Schools.* Accessed January 6, 2020. https://www.primroseschools.com/blog/encouraging-cooperation-with-children/

Kassi, Tara. 2018. "5 Hard Truths to Teach Children about Leadership." *DesignEDly: Intentionally designed resources to engage, empower, and inspire educators.* (2018, February 21). Accessed January 6, 2020. https://mydesignedly.com/5-hard-truths-to-teach-children-about-leadership/

Kassi, Tara. 2017. "How to Maximize Your Student Interest Inventory to Reach Your Most Challenging Students." *DesignEDly: Intentionally designed resources to engage, empower, and inspire educators.* (2017, July 28). Accessed January 22, 2020. https://mydesignedly.com/how-to-maximize-your-student-interest-inventory-to-reach-your-most-challenging-students/

Kearney, Elizabeth PhD. 1996. "Collegial Planning in Classroom Discipline in the Elementary Schools in the Archdiocese of Omaha." PhD dissertation. University of New England.

Kohn, Alfie. 1993. *Punished by Rewards.* New York, NY: Houghton Mifflin Co.

Kravitz, Zalman Rabbi. "Maimonides' Eight Levels of Charity." *Jews for Judaism.* Accessed January 26, 2020. https://jewsforjudaism.org/knowledge/articles/maimonides-eight-levels-charity

Lickona, Dr. Thomas. 1985. *Raising Good Children.* U.S.A., Banton Books.

Popova, Maria. "How Long It Takes to Form a New Habit." (2014, January 2). Accessed 20 February 2020. *BrainPickings.* < https://www.brainpickings.org/2014/01/02/how-long-it-takes-to-form-a-new-habit/>.

"Punishment." *Merriam-Webster.com Dictionary*, Merriam-Webster. Accessed February 18, 2020. <https://www.merriam-webster.com/dictionary/punishment.

Piaget, Jean and Margaret Cook (translator). 1952. *The Origins of Intelligence in Children.* New York, NY: W.W. Norton & Co.

Przybocki, Christine. 2019. *Climbing to the Moon.* USA: *Discipline with Purpose* (self-published).

Rasmussen, Greta. 1989. *Play by the Rules: Creative Practice in Direction Following.* USA: Tin Man Press.

Rymanowicz, Kylie. "Screen Time for Young Children." *Michigan State University.* (2018, March 6). Accessed March 11, 2020. https://www.canr.msu.edu/news/screen_time_for_young_children.

Schawbel, Dan and John Lee Dumas. 2016. "How Leaders Can Set the Right Goals." *Forbes* SMART. (2016, January 17). Accessed January 26, 2020. https://www.forbes.com/sites/danschawbel/2016/01/17/john-lee-dumas-how-leaders-can-set-the-right-goals/#415c7abf376a

Small Talk Big Results. 2010. "Use FORM to Keep the Conversation Going!" (2010, August 23). Accessed January 26, 2020. https://smalltalkbigresults.wordpress.com/2010/08/23/use-form-to-keep-the-conversation-going/

Tanner, Laurel N. 1978. *Classroom Discipline: For effective teaching and learning:* New York, NY: Holt, Rinehart, and Winston.

Tanner, Laurel N. Dr. *New York Times.* (2013, October 25). Accessed January 21, 2020. https://archive.nytimes.com/query.nytimes.com/gst/fullpage-9C01E3DD103AF936A15753C1A9659D8B63.html

"Teaching Cooperative Skills." 1998. *InTime.* University of Northern Iowa. Accessed January 26, 2020. https://intime.uni.edu/teaching-cooperative-skills

Vasiloff, Barbara. 1982. "The Teacher's Vital Role in Developing Student Discipline." *Momentum* (December). 23-26.

Vasiloff, Barbara. 1982. "In-Service Workshop: A Positive Approach." *Today's Catholic Teacher.* 31-34.

Vasiloff, Barbara. 1983. "Discipline: The Challenge of the 80's." *Today's Catholic Teacher.* 32-34.

Vasiloff, Barbara. 1995. *Tips Everyone Can Use to Teach the Skills. Discipline with Purpose.*

Vasiloff, Barbara. 1997. "Don't Just Discipline, Teach Self-Discipline." *Today's Catholic Teacher.* (October) 15-17.

Vasiloff, Barbara. 2003. *Teaching Self-Discipline to Children: 15 Essential Skills.* Mystic: Connecticut: Twenty-Third Publications.

Vasiloff, Barbara. 2005. "Discipline Begins with 'Disciples'." *Religion Teacher's Journal.* (September). 11.

Vasiloff, Barbara. 2006. "The Answer to Good Questions." *Religion Teacher's Journal.* (January) 17-18.

Vasiloff, Barbara. 2006. "Teaching Self-Discipline Skills." *Religion Teacher's Journal.* (February) 21.

Vasiloff, Barbara. 2006. "Building Social Skills." *Religion Teacher's Journal.* (March) 7.

Vasiloff, Barbara. 2006. "Increasing Participation with Communication Skills." *Religion Teacher's Journal* (April/May,) 28.

Vasiloff, Barbara. "*Discipline with Purpose:* Lesson plans for Pre-K students." www.selfdisciplinedwp.com located in shopping cart item #140.

Vasiloff, Barbara. *Discipline with Purpose.* Accessed January 26, 2020. http://www.selfdisciplinedwp.com

Vasiloff, Barbara. *Discipline with Purpose:* Lesson plans for Grades 4-8. www.selfdisciplinedwp.com located in the shopping cart item #141.

Volpitta, Donna EdD and Joel Haber PhD. 2012. *The Resilience Formula.* USA: NW Widener Publishers.

Washington, George. 2013. *110 Rules of Civility and Decent Behavior.* Rowman & Littlefield Publishers. Lanam, Maryland.

"William James on the Psychology of Habit." *Brain Pickings.* Accessed January 26, 2020. https://www.brainpickings.org/2012/09/25/william-james-on-habit/

Wolfgang, Charles and Carl Glickman, 1980. *Solving Discipline Problems.* Massachusetts: Ally and Bacon, Inc.

Appendix

12 Principles of Classroom Discipline

Tanner, Laurel N. 1978. *Classroom Discipline: For effective teaching and learning*. New York, NY: Holt, Rinehart, and Winston.

1. The aims of education and classroom discipline are the same: to help children and youth become self-directed persons.
2. Discipline should be dynamic, helping pupils channel their energies toward learning goals.
3. Discipline is inseparable from teaching.
4. Discipline should change with the child's stage of development and help him move to the next step.
5. Appropriate behavior is determined by the rational demands of specific situations.
6. Teaching effectiveness, as perceived by pupils, invests the teacher with classroom authority.
7. Discipline is the ability to attend to a task.
8. No matter what the classroom design or how pupils are organized for instruction, the principles for effective teaching and discipline apply.
9. By identifying and dealing effectively with the factors under their control and influence, teachers can, in most cases, tip the ecological balance in favor of discipline.
10. Socialization requires the redirection of destructive behavior into socially useful behavior.
11. Ways of dealing with misbehavior should be consonant with developmental goals.
12. Basic discipline can be achieved only when basic needs, such as food and safety, are gratified.

Kindergarten Readiness

- Speak so a non-family member can understand them
- Leave a parent or guardian for a long period of time without have a traumatic experience.
- Play beside and with other children.
- Make simple choices.
- Initiate leisure time activities.

- Can draw a picture to express an idea.
- Recognize and try to write their name.
- Begin to connect letter sounds to letters (such as the sound of the first letter in her name) https://www.understood.org/en/learning-attention-issues/child-learning-disabilities/reading-issues/phonological-awareness-what-it-is-and-how-it-works
- Manage bathroom needs without assistance.
- Dress themselves.
- Sit through an age-appropriate story.
- Understand that the consequences of their actions can cause pain or sadness or happiness and joy to others.
- Treat others in a respectful manner.

Kindergarten Readiness Test found on https://www.understood.org/en/learning-thinking-differences/signs-symptoms/academic-readiness/skills-kids-need-going-into-kindergarten.

Reported Results of Using Discipline with Purpose for Three or More Years

1. There was a dramatic drop in the number of office referrals.
2. Teachers, students, and parents developed a common understanding of the differences between discipline and self-discipline, all school and classroom rules, classroom and total school discipline plans, the 15 self-discipline skills, and how they look/sound in action.
3. Students began to practice self-discipline skills on their own without prompts.
4. Groups of students were able to quickly maintain focused listening during assemblies and in classes.
5. Consistent language and consistent expectations were used when talking about student performance and behavioral challenges.
6. Illustrations of the skills were posted throughout the school building as visual reminders of the behaviors expected.
7. Parents noticed the skills were practiced at home. Children shared what they had learned with others.
8. Teachers were able to use their preferred teaching style and incorporate existing discipline programs into the fifteen-skill framework.
9. The culture of the school was defined in pre-teaching checklists which give unity and direction to all school and classroom activities.

10. There was more staff unity and cohesiveness. The staff held one another accountable for modeling the skills.

A Sample of Items Included in the Rules of Civility – George Washington

Colonial America - Scholastic Professional Books

In the presence of others sing not to yourself with a humming noise, nor drum with your fingers or feet.

Sleep not when others speak, sit not when others stand. Speak not when you should hold your peace, walk not on when others stop.

Turn not your back to others especially in speaking. Jog not the table or desk on which another reads or writes, lean not upon anyone.

Keep our nails clean and short, also your hands and teeth clean yet without showing any great concern for them.

Show not yourself glad at the misfortune of another though he were your enemy.

Do not laugh too loud or too much at any public spectacle.

If anyone come to speak to you while you are sitting, stand up though he be your inferior.

Whisper not in the company of others.

Speak not evil of the absent for it is unjust.

Being set at meal scratch not neither spit cough or blow your nose except there's a necessity for it.

Blow not your broth at Table but stay till cools of itself. Put not your meat to your mouth with your knife in your hand neither spit forth the stones of any fruit pie upon a dish nor cast anything under the table.

About the Author

Barbara Vasiloff is an author, educator, entrepreneur, and co-founder/program developer of *Discipline with Purpose.* She has been an educational consultant for the past 35 years.

Barbara holds a Masters of Arts Degree from Creighton University in Omaha, NE and a Bachelor of Science in Education from the College of St. Teresa in Winona, MN. She has over 40 years teaching experience in elementary, high school, college, and adult education and has taught in both public and private schools in Washington, D.C., Utah, New Mexico, Minnesota, and Nebraska.

Barbara is a contributing author to several national publications and has lectured throughout the United States on the topic of self-discipline. Her previous book, *Teaching Self-Discipline to Children* has been disseminated internationally. She has also co-authored several books dealing with Alzheimer's Disease.

To learn more, please visit www.selfdisciplinedwp.com.